PRAISE FOR DIONYSIAN BUDDHISM

"Claudio Naranjo is one of the most important pioneers of consciousness and human potential. His explorations ranged from Gestalt therapy to psychedelics, from the Enneagram—which he introduced to the United States—to meditation, and from myths to education. This remarkable volume contains powerful guidance for seekers, and reflects Naranjo's gift for creative synthesis and integration of diverse traditions."

— Alfonso Montuori, PhD, California Institute of Integral Studies

"Claudio Naranjo was a visionary in the study of psychology and personality and a profound teacher of spiritual insights and practices. In *Dionysian Buddhism*, Naranjo gives us a gift usually reserved for his students: guided and partnered meditations delivered with poetic and celestial simplicity. He invites readers to disappear into infinity, practice panoramic attention, and meet pain with joy, inspiring a rigorous contemplation that transforms our lives and draws us into compassionate presence with others. Translated by Naranjo himself from recordings of his teachings, the words within reflect the spirit of his company. Through this book, his wise instruction and heartfelt legacy live on."

— Rick Doblin, Founder and Executive Director of The Multidisciplinary
   Association for Psychedelic Studies (MAPS)

"Claudio has always been an inner explorer, and here he invites us to join him. In these many meditations and revelations, we can explore for ourselves the benefit of Claudio's unique expression at the heart of Buddhist practice."

— Jack Kornfield, Author of *A Path With Heart*

"A remarkable and surprising book! This powerful collection of meditations offered by my old friend Claudio Naranjo is a treasure house of awakening."

— Roshi Joan Halifax, Abbot, Upaya Zen Center

"*Dionysian Buddhism* is a wonderful addition to Claudio Naranjo's literary opus. It is a unique book that conveys the atmosphere, clarity, and compassion of Claudio's work as a meditation teacher for decades beginning in the U.S. and Spain, later giving trainings around the globe. Readers who never met Claudio during his lifetime will understand from this book why so many individuals taught by Claudio later said: Meeting Claudio Naranjo changed my life."

— Iven Lourie, Senior Editor, Gateways Books and Tapes, author of poetry
   collections *Miro's Dream* and *Return to Mykonos*

T0151242

"In *Dionysian Buddhism*, Naranjo's poetic instructions lead us effortlessly through a series of meditations that reflect the historical stages of Buddhism as a philosophy—each meditation more profound than the last. This book belongs on the bookshelf (if not on the shrine) of every Western Buddhist."

— Mike Crowley, Author of *Secret Drugs of Buddhism: Psychedelics Sacraments and the Origins of the Vajrayana*

"Claudio Naranjo brings his characteristic intelligence and depth of knowledge to the three major Buddhist schools, helping us understand the meditation practices of each from a historical and philosophical perspective and shedding light on their core principles. With his brilliant synthesizing capacity, he simultaneously adds an interpersonal dimension to the typically intrapersonal practice of meditation."

— Sandra Maitri, author of *The Spiritual Dimension of the Enneagram: Nine Faces of the Soul* & *The Enneagram of Passions and Virtues: Finding the Way Home*

"As an expansive and innovative thinker, Claudio understood well that this rapidly changing world is in need of deep personal and intra-personal healing. Impermanence today reveals itself in more radical and unpredictable ways than ever before and cultivating balance and harmony is the most important work we can do. Here, Claudio makes a unique contribution—I cherish this opportunity to express my appreciation for such a luminary, who dedicated his life to wisdom and understanding."

— Tarthang Tulku Rinpoche, Founder of The Nyingma Institute

"This masterful compilation guides individuals and partners in meditation by means of many ingenuous aphorisms that were originally spoken to groups at the very moment of entering into meditative states. It presents, in Claudio Naranjo's skillfully selected words, that he proved to be effective in leading minds beyond words. In this book I have, at last, found his teaching articulated."

— David Stophlet Flattery, Author of *Catalyst of Miracles: The Unknown Claudio Naranjo*

"Through the ancient wisdom of Theravada Buddhism and Naranjo's clear and unambiguous guidance, we discover—or rediscover—both happiness and despair, holding fast to our gratitude and beginning to look deeply at what is beneath our suffering, refreshing our meditative practice and compelling us toward a path of emanating care."

— Allan Badiner, Editor of *Zig Zag Zen: Buddhism and Psychedelics*

Dionysian
Buddhism

Dionysian Buddhism

*Guided Interpersonal Meditations
in the Three Yanas*

CLAUDIO NARANJO

SYNERGETIC PRESS
SANTA FE • LONDON

Synergetic Press | 1 Bluebird Court, Santa Fe, NM 87508 & 24 Old Gloucester St. London, WC1N 3AL England

Library of Congress Cataloging-in-Publication Data

Names: Naranjo, Claudio, author.
Title: Dionysian Buddhism : guided interpersonal meditations in the Three Yanas / Claudio Naranjo.
Description: First. | Santa Fe : Synergetic Press, 2022. | Summary: "Dionysian Buddhism: Guided Interpersonal Meditations in the Three Yanas will assist readers in exploring their own emotional landscapes. This sequence of thirty guided meditations by the renowned spiritual teacher and psychotherapist Claudio Naranjo is structured to guide individuals towards acceptance of what is and to be fully present -- to meet pain with joy, expand awareness into consciousness and to learn how to share in the full presence of others. The "Dionysian" context of Buddhism provides a lens in which to interpret non-attachment through noninterference with the stream of life. Naranjo draws on a wide range of Buddhist traditions, from Theravada to Vajrayana, in order to create a work that emphasizes both the experiential and multifaceted aspects of meditation. As Naranjo says, "Only a change of consciousness might save our world, and that in view of this collective shift in consciousness there is nothing more relevant we can do than start with ourselves.""-- Provided by publisher.
Identifiers: LCCN 2022002474 (print) | LCCN 2022002475 (ebook) | ISBN 9780907791973 (paperback) | ISBN 9780907791980 (ebook)
Subjects: LCSH: Buddhist meditations. | Meditation. | Theravāda Buddhism.
Classification: LCC BQ5572 .N37 2022 (print) | LCC BQ5572 (ebook) | DDC 294.3/4432--dc23/eng/20220129
LC record available at https://lccn.loc.gov/2022002474
LC ebook record available at https://lccn.loc.gov/2022002475
ISBN: 9780907791973 (paperback)
ISBN: 9780907791980 (ebook)

Cover design by Amanda Müller
Book design by Howie Severson
Managing Editor: Amanda Müller
Project Editor: Noelle Armstrong
Printed in the USA

Dedicated with gratitude to Tarthang Tulku Rinpoche, who about four decades ago told me that I would liberate myself and yet has been a guru to me beyond any other.

Table of Contents

Editor's Note

After decades of teaching in person, Claudio Naranjo began to record his meditations and insights for transcription in a Spanish edition of this text, *Budismo Dionisiaco: Meditaciones Guiadas*, originally published by Ediciones La Llave in 2013. The English rendition you are holding was translated by Claudio himself—for this reason, we have tried to preserve much of the unique word choice and punctuation rather than revising toward a more traditional syntax. These choices pay tribute to the cadence of his speech, a multilingual worldview, and poetic style that evoke his physical presence and reflect the feeling of studying in person with this one-of-a-kind spiritual teacher.

Preface

For a long time I have resisted the request to put together in book form the transcripts of the meditations I have been teaching (always in an improvised manner and always somewhat differently) year after year during the SAT (Seekers After Truth) program. On the one hand, I have thus far preferred that such meditations be a privilege for my students, who participate in person in this multifaceted program that has involved not only an introduction to the three yanas of Buddhist meditation but also a systematic process of self-knowledge, body work, and other ingredients. On the other hand, I felt that in merely presenting variations on the classic techniques of Buddhism, such meditations did not contain enough novelty to merit that I present them in a book under my name.

In regard to my first objection I feel differently today, however, being close to 82, and want to leave a written record of my contributions to the various specialties I have cultivated. And I have also been feeling differently about the notion that what I have done is not so innovative; firstly because in my way of teaching traditional meditation I have always wanted to emphasize the essential issues through a diversity of formal variations and also because, although I initially limited my explanations to brief preliminary talks before the sessions (during which I remained silent, as is customary), I have more recently presented my remarks on the practice during the sessions themselves, which have thus taken on the character of guided meditations.

The interpersonal, intersubjective, or relational context in which I have embedded the well-known techniques of the Buddhist schools is also original to my presentation, in proposing that people sit facing each other in (rotating) pairs throughout the duration of each sitting and that the meditation sessions start with eyes closed, continue with open eyes, and then proceed (during the final part of each meditation) to silent eye-to-eye contact. Because I've always kept in mind that deep meditation is contagious and because I believe face-to-face encounters involve the potential for transmission or inspiration, I have wanted to take advantage of such an opportunity in a systematic way.

When I designed the SAT (Seekers After Truth) Program during the late Eighties in Spain, I decided that during the first module I would focus on the legacy of the Theravada tradition, during the second module on Zazen (and something about its corresponding cultural context), and during the third module I would concentrate on some contributions of the Tibetan tradition. Over time, however, two short modules were added to the original SAT Program, in which I have presented further supplements to the body of these meditations: on the one hand, a form of devotional practice based, not on the invocation or visualization of deities, but in hearing classical music as mind-transmissions from the contemplative experience of great composers. Also, an introduction to the Theravada practice of the Jhanas and some meditations originated outside Buddhism and yet coherent with Buddhist experience (a series of reflections on death and a new perspective on time that I have borrowed from Eckhart Tolle).

I have often asked those coming to the fourth module of my program, "What form of meditation do I teach?," and have been surprised to find that it has not been easy for my students to answer my question. They have frequently said "Vipassana," or "doing nothing," and sometimes "seeing everything from space," but it has rarely occurred to them to simply answer "Buddhist meditation," which is what I've always tried to do (particularly since, thanks to Yogi Chen, I understood the Nyingmapa proposition of integrating all yanas). An even more accurate answer, however, would be that I have taught "Buddhism in a Dionysian context" and my meditation sessions are part of a therapeutic enterprise that transmits an implicit faith in instinct and in spontaneity (strongly reinforced in my programs through the practice of "spontaneous movement": an exercise of surrender to what happens in us "by itself" when we allow our mind to be free). In regard to this Dionysian context, I can say that—in my way of presenting meditation—I have been very aware of the notion of a complementarity between not-doing and allowing the free flow of mental activity. That is to say, between controlling our mind and letting go of its control and also between two complementary ways of non-attachment: an ("Apollonian") renunciation of impulses and a ("Dionysian") noninterference with the stream of life.

While editing the transcripts included in this volume I have endeavored to use the arrangement of the words on the page to give an idea of the timing of my remarks in which periods of seconds or minutes alternate with longer ones.

I launch this book into the world with the hope that my transcribed words can go beyond those that I have written by my own hand, which have addressed so far the more abstract or theoretical aspects of meditation (such as the common ground and complementarities between meditation and psychotherapy).

Just as during the Sixties we witnessed a true explosion of interest in meditation in California, it seems to me that today (at the end of the millennium) the most visible explosion has been an interest in survival and money, so that there has been little new food to stimulate the spiritual search of seekers. I hope, therefore, that this book will bring some self-perfecting stimulus to those who feel so busy and tired that they can no longer think about pilgrimages or the search for new teachers.

It may be that some of my readers share my conviction that only a change of consciousness might save our world and that, in view of this collective shift in consciousness, there is nothing more relevant we can do than start with ourselves. I end, therefore, by offering them the encouragement of considering that meditation is not only helpful to ourselves, but also our psychosocial environment, as we go through a most critical time.

Why Buddhist Meditation?

Having been a thirsty seeker who has passed through the main spiritual schools, one might imagine that in teaching meditation I would integrate elements from various sources; yet I long ago decided to focus on the legacy of Buddhism, just as I have also focused, for decades, on the practice of Buddhist meditation on my personal journey.

Virtually every spiritual tradition practices some form of meditation and some traditions teach several. But it can be said of none of them as much as it is said of Buddhism that it is a "religion of meditation."

As it can be said that Christianity is a religion of Love or Judaism a religion of Law, that Confucianism constitutes a religion of right relationships, or that Taoism is a religion of spontaneity, and Islam a religion of surrender, it may be said of Buddhism that its distinctive emphasis is on the optimization of the mind.

While in the Abrahamic religions, contact with the divine is sought through prayer, Buddhism has emphasized the view that what we seek has been always present, although our mind has been too busy with its thoughts and desires for us to perceive it. And what the Buddhist tradition proposes as purification and cultivation of the mind is a great synthesis that includes India's yogic past, the relationship between the Eightfold Path of Buddhism, and the eightfold yoga of Patanjali, resembling the relationship between the Mosaic and Christian religions: a transfer of a vintage wine into new wineskins. Also, in addition to the timeless inspiration of yoga, Buddhism integrates Taoist and shamanic elements with the fruits of a continuous evolution—for, unlike Christianity, which closed its scriptural canon in the fourth century, Tibetan Buddhism continues to add to its canon the contributions from the living Buddhas of each generation.

When Western culture became interested in Buddhist meditation, it was mainly the Zen tradition that caught its attention, but later the virtually boundless treasures of Tibetan Buddhism became accessible and more recently the practices and explanations of ancient Theravada Buddhism are being adopted in medicine, psychotherapy, and education.

Although Orthodox Theravadin think that the Mahayana was a deviation from the true doctrine preached by Buddha, and even some Mahayanists have similarly considered Vajrayana Buddhism a deviation from authentic Buddhism, I think Vajrayana Buddhism (which we now associate closely with Tibet) constitutes the most comprehensive synthesis, from which I have adopted the proposition that the teaching of Buddhist meditation should begin with the Satipatthana Sutta, proceed on to the Mahayana, and be completed with the more advanced teachings of Mahamudra and Dzogchen. For that reason, this book includes an experiential journey through Buddhist meditation that begins with an introduction to the practices of quieting and sharpening the mind in the Theravada tradition, continues with a brief experiential introduction to Zen, and ends with a series of meditations intended to communicate the convergence of stillness and clarity in the service of phenomenological research of the mind beyond mental phenomena—as in the Mahamudra.

It goes without saying that, as I have explained in my foreword, I take many liberties through all these guided meditations. Even if I teach what I have understood from the teachings I have received, my words—just from the fact I speak out of personal experience—will be different from those of other written descriptions of meditation.

Something about the Theravada Tradition and Something Further on the Notion of "Dionysian Buddhism"

My introduction to Buddhist practice took place in the late Sixties through sitting with Suzuki Roshi, but I did not feel qualified to teach until after an enlightening experience reached in a very different context: a solitary retreat where I had been sent by Oscar Ichazo, a Bolivian who described himself as "a representative of the Western Prophetic Tradition."

Once I felt ready to start guiding others in their psycho-spiritual development, Zazen became one of the ingredients in the repository of practices which I proposed. I did not come to know Vipassana until—over the course of the first year of meeting with my followers (the group that ultimately became the SAT school) —I met, on Alan Watts' houseboat, a monk from Thailand called Dhiravamsa, who was visiting from England for a few days. I invited him to visit my Berkeley group and this he did, not only on the following day, but for several years, during which he also became known in town and offered many independent workshops in California (which I would also attend in the course of the early Seventies).

Later, I met other Vipassana instructors, such as Rina Sirkar (at the time associated with the California Institute of Integral Studies or CIIS), then a Burmese teacher who visited San Francisco for a season (who was given the dignity of Sayadaw but whose name I forget), and in the end, Goenka. But by then I had already started my training in Tibetan Buddhism and over time it was my personal development under the influence of my root Lama that gave the most shape to my teachings as a meditation instructor.

As I have already mentioned, it was in accordance with the Nyingmapa notion of an integrative pedagogy of meditation that I next designed the International SAT Program, so that its three successive modules included introductory courses in meditation on Buddhism's three levels of teaching that relates mythically to the "Three Turnings of the Wheel of Dharma"[1]; except that, as I have already explained, I have taken some liberties, including the presentation of the techniques as guided meditations in an interpersonal or inter-subjective context.

I remember hearing Alan Watts say that all religions had interested him except Theravada Buddhism, and I think that this statement of his was a reflection of a temporary decline in the ancient tradition, which only during the past century has been recovering its spiritual abundance (and has most recently warranted the interest of physicians and others in its presentation as mindfulness). It may be said that orthodox presentations of this old tradition not only deny the value of Mahayana and the validity of Vajrayana, but rely excessively on revulsion and contempt for the body in their pedagogy of non-attachment. Yet this approach has the virtue of focusing on the original issues of Buddhism—such as the emphasis on attention, the complementarity of Vipassana and Shamata, and the four Noble Truths—and the simple language of this tradition lends itself very well to our secular and eminently rational culture.

To talk about Dionysian Buddhism may seem inappropriate when we consider the spirit of the Theravada tradition, but it is justified in reference to the inclusion of these classical meditations in a therapeutic context that, unlike the spiritual traditions, affirms the need to transcend the repressive spirit, affirms instinctual life, and proposes that we don't confuse our "animal side" with the neurotic needs resulting from its chronic repression in a patriarchal culture. Such a view seems to me perfectly consistent with the Four Noble Truths but especially with the spirit of Tantric Buddhism, which may very well deserve to be called "Dionysian Buddhism" (or Shiva-like Buddhism, since the Indian Siva and the European Dionysus are the same). Yet the purpose of this book is not theoretical, and I now move on to the first series of meditation transcripts.

---

1 The Three Turnings of the Wheel of Dharma are:
1. The Four Noble Truths (cattari ariya saccani), relating to Hinayana
2. Universal no-thing-ness (shunyata), relating to early Mahayana
3. The Buddha-nature (tathagatagarbha) of all beings, relating to late Mahayana

I

Theravada Variations

1

Sweet Doing Nothing in Relation

Before giving you the first instructions about how to meditate, I want to invite you to try to improve the state of your own mind by just using your intuition.

I have started with this instruction because I am sure that we all have in us the potential to be guided in our meditation by our deeper wisdom, and that, beyond the many formulas that we may learn, we should not lose our natural ability to improvise.

But now I will give you a first instruction, or formula: Do nothing.

Doing nothing is like receiving grace: sometimes it happens, and sometimes it doesn't. To do nothing at all may sometimes be like falling into a bottomless depth.

If I allow myself to do nothing, I can enter a mysterious space beyond thought.

But sometimes we cannot go beyond our incessant and habitual thinking. And thinking, of course, is not "doing nothing."

If we want to stop thinking, it may be helpful to observe our thinking process.

As a step towards silence, then, we may not just observe what thoughts we are generating, but what moves us to do so.

For the mind that watches thoughts is not the thinking mind.

Yet perhaps it is even better that we tire of thinking, and we tire of thinking when we are disenchanted by its results.

We need to be disappointed by our thinking mind to detach from it, and then become more interested in silence.

Also, the very familiar Italian idea of "dolce far niente" (sweet doing nothing) may inspire us to put our thinking mind to rest, since an impulse toward "sweet rest," in which we leave behind the stress of daily life, is already within us, and as much as we are excited by what we do, we may learn to enjoy tossing aside the weight of the mundane, with its concerns and expectations.

Once we stop feeling obliged to deal with this or that, we may enter into a state of peace, and peace also brings us to a state of pleasure, for when we let ourselves drop towards our center, we feel as if we are coming home.

Another aid in getting to "do nothing" is breathing.

Simply observe your breath.

We feel less inclined to think when we are being aware of our breath.

Sometimes it is enough that we feel our breath at every moment, to feel disinclined to think.

It also helps us to go beyond the usual consciousness that we trust, allowing our mind to go wherever it wills, or to entertain the intuition so that, by allowing our mind go where it chooses, a regenerative process of spontaneous healing may take place, just as it happens in the course of restful sleep.

Just as while we sleep we renew our energy, relaxing our thoughts allows a subtle regenerative activity in which everything is heading towards where it belongs: a self-regulating activity of our inner world, which knows better than our rational mind what it is we need.

So even if we don't know how to become happier, all we need is to let ourselves sink, releasing control, letting ourselves simply dissolve.

I invite you now to keep a silent mind with open eyes, without looking into each other's eyes, but at each other's solar plexuses.

Seeing rather than looking, allowing incoming visual perceptions, with no intention of doing anything with them.

The experience of being with eyes open and not thinking may be less familiar than that of not thinking with closed eyes.

It may even feel that it is dangerous to be in the world without thinking, or facing another without preparing to say something, or without preparing to react to what another says or does. And having your eyes open helps with being more awake or attentive, just as being attentive helps us not forget the task of mental silence.

But if you find it difficult to silence the mind, observe the inner dialogues that you entertain.

What is it you are thinking, and where does it come from?
Does your thinking deserve the attention it is demanding?

If not, such a realization may help you drop it.

It may be that the presence of another serves to calm your thoughts, but it may also happen that the interpersonal situation makes inner silence harder, for we fail to stop imagining how the other sees us, or feels about us.

If so, let us again seize the opportunity to observe our thoughts, and, having observed them, test whether we are able to sit face to face in true silence, mindful of our breathing and detaching from all purpose.

What do we feel, then?

I invite you now to share in pairs for a few minutes about what you have experienced during this experiment of silent contact.

2

An Introduction to Vipassana

The word Vipassana refers to clarity, and has been translated into English as *insight*, though in reference to a very different kind of insight than the same term in psychoanalytical or therapeutic discourse, where it refers to an understanding of emotions, motivations, or psychological processes.

The understanding sought through Vipassana does not refer to what happens in our psychological world, and might be called "philosophical insight" if the term "philosophical" did not usually refer to the kind of understanding that results from discursive or rational activity.

The insight that rewards a successful practitioner of Vipassana is not intellectual, but an experiential grasp of certain truths about all experience that constitute characteristic teachings of Buddhism: Dukkha or unsatisfactoriness, Anicca or impermanence, and Anatta or absence of self.

As we will see, in Tibetan Buddhism the term Vipassana refers more specifically to a practice in which the aim is to discover the nature of the subject of experience, consciousness, or as it is said, "the nature of the mind" beyond mental phenomena. The Theravada tradition has come to call Vipassana a simple observation of the experience of the present moment with equanimity—as set forth in the Sutta of The Four Foundations of Mindfulness (Satipatthana Sutta): mindfulness of body, mindfulness of feelings, mindfulness of impulses, and mindfulness of consciousness—all of which are most commonly today called simply "mindfulness" by the professionals in psychology and education.

During these sessions, we will practice paying attention to our experience of the moment or to certain aspects of it, understanding that in exercising this kind of clarity of perception of the immediate we are laying the foundation for the exercise of directing this sharpened attention toward the very center of our consciousness. There we discover a kind of nothingness that the Theravada tradition describes as a non-self and Mahayana designates as Reality, Sunyata (or emptiness), or Buddhahood. This is an experience that implies a felt understanding that our daily self is not our true identity, and that we harbor in us a deeper, arguably cosmic, identity.

There are those who come to this insight through the simple practice of mindfulness or through the practice of not-doing, but the ancient tradition recommends the simultaneous cultivation of both, and this is also the case in Tibetan Buddhism.

As you can imagine, a vivid understanding of the illusory nature of our human identity can lead the successful practitioner to a condition where he can finally leave behind all his problems. (One of my teachers—Oscar Ichazo—used to quote his own master who would tell him, in response to his impatience, "Wait, until you understand you do not exist, and then you will stop worrying about such things").

Vipassana can lead us to another aspect of insight called Dukkha, which is usually translated as "suffering," with a more accurate translation of "dissatisfaction" or "unsatisfactoriness."

The first of the Four Noble Truths of Buddhism—commonly called "the truth of suffering"—is usually explained quite rationally. It is said, for example, that our life is fleeting and is heading towards the decrepitude of old age or that our desires are always greater than the possible satisfaction we can expect to get, which is always ephemeral, etc. But I think the understanding of the famous "truth of suffering" is something different from such reasoning and should instead be compared to what in the psychological culture of our time we call "the truth of neurosis." We suffer for the loss of our mental health even while only vaguely realizing it so that, in our alienation, we don't even realize that we have lost the perception that our life has a meaning beyond survival or the satisfaction of desires.

In Buddhism the vocabulary is different, and it is said that our consciousness has lost its clarity, so that we live lives comparable to those of sleepwalkers who do not know they are half asleep as they roam the Samsara—an expression that refers to walking in circles.

But even though not all those affected by an emotional pathology (which all virtually are) realize their lack, some do become aware of their condition and, even though they suffer for it, seek their healing. In the Buddhist path some discover that behind their worldly love and work satisfaction they are left with an aftertaste of insubstantiality or insufficiency. And although our friends and even our doctor may draw our attention to a short-lived psychological problem, perhaps our malaise involves a glimpse of our condition of incompleteness, ignorance, and chronic dysfunction. That we do not feel fulfilled, then, is not just a "psychological problem" but a vague awareness that we are in the dark, having lost our North and our light, so that, having lost our way, we live false lives.

Before undertaking the practice of meditation, we may be satisfied with ourselves and delighted with our thoughts. We feel intelligent and every thought we produce carries the illusion that our next thought will provide us in turn with a future satisfaction. But with the practice of self-observation, we come to feel that our thinking is rather like the activity of a not-so-remarkable thinking machine. Even though it exceeds a computer in some respects, at the end of the day it's just a thinking machine and— if we were too excited about our cognitive capacity—it is foreseeable that we will suffer some disappointment.

This is also true about our emotional mechanisms. Initially we feel our emotional world is something profound, but it is more accurate to say that it is intense, and we eventually come to understand that the emotional field is also subject to mechanisms and programs that make it predictable. We have an emotional repertoire with which we respond to the world, but even if it contains all the colors of the rainbow, wouldn't this not indicate that, much as a carousel in its movement causes its seats or horses to rise, our emotions also follow a kind of mechanism that causes them to rise or fall cyclically?

And has the Freudian vision of the mind not been compared to hydraulics, an alternative to the mechanics of solids?

Also, the animal parts of our mind—our sexuality, aggression, desires—with their peculiar intensity, may become less important to us as the practice of meditation diminishes our attachment, leading us to some measure of frustration-tolerance and even arguably the beginning of wisdom, so that we are no longer so delighted with the world of simple pleasures, which trapped us before we became interested in reaching another dimension of consciousness. Also, it is part of the Dharma—or teachings or Buddhist faith—to assert that everything is transitory, and that the transitory and ephemeral cannot give us the satisfaction of feeling *what is*.

It is therefore recommended in Buddhism to cultivate the awareness of our own mortality, which leads to not waste so much time. Life is best used if we are aware of how precious an opportunity it is—particularly for the possibility of working toward our own evolution.

When we were young it seemed we would have time for everything, and we could get it all done, but as time passes by, our possibilities become more limited, so that we must give up some things. Also, not wanting to waste so much time in a "horizontal" exploration of "more of the same," we become more interested in a spiritual dimension—concerned with the depth of our experience of the moment.

Such, then, are the things that come to be understood through what the Theravadins call Vipassana: the universality of suffering as a background to life, the universality of impermanence, which makes everything (including our very lives) fleeting, and the illusoriness of self as something solid and permanent, rather than simply a transitory state.

I hope that in making its purpose explicit I may be stirring your motivation to practice, for meditation is something like the laboratory of the teachings, and without the light of the teachings it is easy for Vipassana to seem pointless and become boring—as long as insight is not reached, being "here and now" is not an ecstatogenic activity. On the contrary, being with the breathing while sensing and observing useless thoughts may become difficult at times for beginners to endure.

Yet not necessarily, since not only in the Christian world but in the Buddhist world there is a knowledge of Grace, and even beginners may sometimes discover the present to be a gateway to infinity.

But this gateway is not discovered through anticipation of the future or a remembrance of the past and we must find a way to be in the present with our thinking silenced, dropping the notion of going somewhere or attaining anything. Then we may come to know that in spite of the impermanence of all things, desires, and thoughts, there is an awareness that we might not be able to say *exists*—and yet is the basis of everything—like an empty and all-encompassing background of our mind.

But I leave this introduction now and invite you to the practice, which today will be, in addition to the instruction to "do nothing," that of attending to the experience of the present. By way of preparation for this experience of the present, it may be useful to consider something that we already know well, although we live as if we don't know it—the past no longer exists except in our memory (which consists of the present activity of evoking it) and that the future also doesn't exist (except in our present mental activity of anticipating it).

Our basic exercise in Vipassana is "being in the present" but, as we will see, it is not as easy as it might seem to be in the present, for we are tempted to shift mentally into the past or the future. Thus, let us describe what we will now attempt as "renouncing anticipation and memory."

And if before we begin we remind ourselves that neither the past nor the future exists, this renunciation may perhaps not be so difficult for us to achieve.

3

Panoramic Attention and Transparent Presence

When we pay attention to the present we understand that every
moment of our consciousness is multidimensional.
There is in our experience a bodily aspect and, simultaneously, we
hear the sounds of our surroundings.

And we can feel ourselves breathing,
And we perceive a certain emotional atmosphere:
perhaps we feel good, or maybe not so good ...
and also some thoughts cross our mind, in spite of having decided
to think as little as possible.

We leave the past behind, we give up the future,
and we turn our attention to the present,
endeavoring not to get into a conversation with ourselves,
mindful only of our immediate experiences,
not falling into the temptation of making commentaries
or taking notes about them, so we can recall them later.

We just feel the present in silence.

If we are in the present, and thought does not distract us from
the present, we will surely feel our breathing, and also feel the
subtle pleasure intrinsic to breathing.

The pleasure of breathing conveys a sense of animal simplicity
and nobility, and may resemble aesthetic pleasure in its nearness to
the sense of being.

When we feel okay, feeling our breath may be nourishing,
in that it brings us in contact with something that we cannot
describe as a superficial pleasure
and that we associate with being alive.

The word "psyche," meaning "soul," refers to the breath, or to
the air we breathe, indicating that nothing feels closer to life
than breathing.

Just as it seems to us that as we breathe we absorb life,
it seems that breathing brings us nearer to an invisible life-core
at the center of ourselves.

Let us focus, then, on the beauty of breathing,
which is something like pleasure but also something like the
nobility of life itself,
which we have forgotten—just as we forget our breathing
when we become distracted from ourselves by the world of things,
and by our incessant thoughts and practical worries.
Let us be mindful, then, of the spontaneous pleasure of life
attached to breathing.

Sometimes we are tempted to manipulate our own experience.

We would like to feel something more gratifying and we have not
yet understood that meditation is not at all coming to feel something different,
but instead looking at what we are experiencing from a different
angle, or with different eyes.
Perhaps more openly,
or with more acceptance.
For even if Vipassana is explained as a practice of paying attention
to what we experience
moment after moment,
it is also a practice of being okay with what there is.
And since what the present brings us is not necessarily pleasant,
(for at times we feel sadness, boredom, or anger)
it is important that we learn to let our feelings be as they are,
giving them space, and wanting to truly know them,
and not despising them for not being what we would prefer to feel.
The practice of acceptance, too, is a practice of neutrality,
in which we learn to become like a mirror
that holds no preferences in regards to what it is reflecting.

The practice of attention to the present, then, involves being open
and also involves detachment, or non-attachment:
nothing is rejected,
and we try not to hold on to anything.

And we can take breathing as an opportunity to remember
the fundamental task of simply knowing
moment after moment what we are experiencing.
With each breath we make an observation,
Becoming aware of what is happening,
what we feel, how it is to be here at this moment.

We prepare now to open our eyes, but looking down rather than
face-to-face with our partner.

We continue paying attention to each breath, to the emotional tone
of the moment,
to everything that happens, but mainly to what attracts our
attention the most,
coming into its foreground, while the remainder of our impressions
fade into the background.
Is the foreground of attention physical right now?
Perhaps emotional?
When you open your eyes, you add another dimension to the experience of the moment.
We now feel the body, hear sounds, perceive emotional states,
and also receive visual impressions, and we are simultaneously
aware of these three realms to the extent that we allow ourselves
a panoramic awareness.

I invite you now to feel your body, listen to the environmental
sounds, and also pay attention to what you see—on every breath.
And perhaps you will notice that when we look panoramically at all
these facets of our experience, this "choiceless awareness" makes
us more aware of "ourselves" as observers at the center of our
many-faceted world.

Now we prepare to meet through the gaze, and I ask you to consider:
What would it be like if the person before you had full access to
your present experience?

In other words: How would it be if you were transparent to each
other? Would this be acceptable to you?
Would you be comfortable in becoming transparent to the one who
sits in front of you?
Or would you prefer to hide some aspect of what you feel?

I ask you this because, when you are ready for such a "transparent encounter," you may experience something different from solitary meditation practice.

It is possible that something like a contagion of consciousness takes place;

a kind of mental transfusion; and then, when you are no longer locked into yourself,

the encounter becomes more mysterious.

Yet it is not necessary that we purport to do anything other than to be in touch with what happens to us while allowing for the possibility of being seen;

that is to say, aware and open,

as if implicitly sharing moment after moment the reality of the here and now.

4

The Enjoyment of Breath, the Silence of Thought, and Panoramic Attention to the Present Moment

We continue with the Vipassana, and this time not only give up the future and the past, but also try to renounce the comments we usually make about the present. We will try to get rid of the description or the reflection about what we experience.

Let us try to stay alone with what happens; that is, with the experience of the present without added thoughts.

I invite you to find new company once again, because moments of non-verbal encounter not only allow a contagion of attention or energy, but sometimes contribute something more specific.

The equanimity we seek to cultivate in the Vipassana—before what happens from moment to moment—implies a background of not doing, which is not only cultivated separately through the Shamata, but through each session of Vipassana. We establish a background of doing nothing before everything we perceive, and that is what allows detachment.

It is therefore a good start to each session to simply allow yourself to be there.

Just let yourself be at peace.

Usually we are not at peace because our ordinary mind or personality is like a machine that always wants something and prepares to go to some goal.

But if, before we start practicing the Vipassana properly, we take time to do nothing, it helps us recover the calm and lightness of the mind.

It is often said that meditation is like letting the dirty water in a vessel settle, so that the suspended particles that obscure it will slowly fall to the bottom.

As with water, the mind requires time to be clarified.

Only after a time of abandoning all intention do we pay attention to the breath, and not only to the sensation of contact with the air and respiratory movements, but to the subtle emotional aspect of the breath—the pleasure of breathing, which is an almost aesthetic pleasure, which we can alternatively allude to as the beauty of breathing.

We do not always feel this beauty of breathing, but sometimes when we look for it, we find ourselves alone with a heaviness, or with an effort. Breathing is a mirror of our emotional reality and we can recover a healthy attitude toward our experience if we recover the natural rhythm of our breathing. It is important, then, to let our breath find its rhythm, and that implies knowing how to listen to its own will, without subjecting it to our control.

Only we are ill-accustomed to taking control of everything that enters our consciousness. While we sleep, our "inner animal" knows very well how to breathe, but as soon as we put our attention on the breath, we make it ours, and we impose our rhythm, and we do not know to let ourselves breathe. Therefore, we also need time for our breathing to shed our stress, and find, like our mind, the calm of something like not doing, which is something like breathing without breathing: allowing our body spontaneous breathing.

For now we will do no more than this: be in the present, letting our breath be released, and feeling, when this happens, that subtle pleasure of breathing, which is like the pleasure of being alive.

For us to live the present, renunciation of thought is necessary. The renunciation of the future, the renunciation of the past, the renunciation of the commentary.

And when one is in the present, one discovers in the present a vast complexity, as in a polyphonic musical work in which we cannot pay attention to each one of the melodies in counterpoint.

Our experience of the present is multifaceted, since at the same time we feel our body, we perceive the environmental sounds, we attend to the pleasure of breathing, and we surely feel some tiredness, or impatience, or spiritual yearning or some other emotional state.

What should we give our preferential attention to?

Although there are many formulas of the Vipassana, I propose this time what Krishnamurti called choiceless awareness—a free or floating attention that does not choose anything in particular.

I invite you to remain open to everything, practicing panoramic attention.

And you will surely discover that when nothing special is chosen—such as the bodily or the emotional—our attention goes by itself to and fro, just as our breathing moves without our control.

And if we insist on being open to everything—which is not an easy thing (because even in the sound world or in that of bodily sensations we tend to concentrate on this or that, losing receptivity to the totality of our field of experience)—it will lead us to feel more present as subjects of our consciousness, beyond the various mental phenomena as sensations, emotions, desires, or thoughts. In the attempt to simultaneously attend to everything without attending to anything in particular, we find that everything is becoming a bit blurry, but we become more aware of being there—observing what flows for us and in our environment.

With each breath let us remember this formula, which prescribes the enjoyment of the breath, the silence of thought, and the panoramic attention to the present moment.

And if we want greater depth, we can look for it through a greater silence, a greater enjoyment of the breath, a greater attention to the present.

Let us now begin to open our eyes, taking care of the continuity of our attention to our triple task and its background of not doing.

And although it may seem at first to be a sacrifice to open our eyes—for we have learned to lose touch with ourselves—we will discover that with enough attention to the transition to the external world, we can, when opening the eyes, become a little more awake, and by being more awake, we can also achieve greater silence.

Looking at the person's Hara before us, then,
we continue the practice of immersion
in the experience of the present,
without entering into conversation with ourselves
or taking notes mentally
to later remember our experiences.
And we also give up taking advantage of what experience we live.
We simply perceive what we perceive,
and we are satisfied with the simple experience of the present.

And now, getting ready to meet, we are looking up, always without
distracting us from the enjoyment of the breath and panoramic
awareness.

What do we prepare ourselves for? To continue the same practice
without falling into the temptation of masking or hiding
but allowing us intimacy in a situation of contact with
the other.

And if we give up anything, allowing our thinking mind to stop,
time will seem to stop, and only the taste of our own presence
will remain.

5

Disappearing into Infinity

If we had enough time, we would prolong the practice of being in the silent present with the enjoyment of the breath before addressing what I will propose to you now. But since we have only a few brief meditation sessions, I will introduce the whole somewhat prematurely so that you may repeat this sequence at home, taking your time, and staying as long as you need to at each stage. I backtrack, now.

We have started by renouncing the past and the future, concentrating on the present, and then focusing on the enjoyment of the breath. We then renounced commentaries, so as to simply concentrate on the immediate experience.

And now I will invite you again to do the same, only leaving aside the focus on the physical sensations involved in breathing. In other words, I am inviting you to do something that might seem impossible: to attend to the affective and aesthetic aspect of breathing without taking into account its physical aspect.

Let us start, as usual, by doing nothing,
other than observing how it is
when we have not yet begun to meditate.

Then, let us include our breathing
in our awareness of the present,
and pay particular attention to the pleasure of breathing.

Although the present includes diverse impressions,
Let us focus on something very simple:
Just knowing ourselves to be here and now.

The more we progress in meditation,
the simpler it becomes.
It is not like psychotherapy,
where we build bridges between memories or experiences
and understand certain things about ourselves.
Now we simply feel present
and enjoy the present.

And if in the beginning
not to think is a task,
with practice it simply becomes resting.

Like when you wait for a dream at night
and you set out to leave the day behind
with your unfinished tasks.
Just let your inner talking rest
trusting that you will attend to your problems again
some other time.

And even if perhaps we intended to meditate
in a search for happiness
or self-perfection,
now that you meditate,
be sure to renounce all purpose,
for only when you stop
expecting any benefit or result

can you fully taste being there.

Being present should not require any effort,
because we are where we are.
We are even, deep down, well,
even if the surface of our mind is agitated.

Just as in the sea there is movement on the surface,
where many fish swim
while the bottom remains calm,
so the surface of our mind moves
while deep down
lies a naturally calm
but forgotten layer of our being,
that we must recover.

Let us now make the transition
to practice with our eyes open,
always savoring the satisfaction
of letting go of any effort,
all haste,
any concern to produce something
or to get somewhere.

And now begin to raise your gaze
still without thoughts,
until you meet through the gaze
unconcerned
about anything beyond
feeling present.

And now I invite you
to make a new experiment:
disappear.

And I ask you:
can you disappear
without the world also disappearing?

I trust that you have found
that if you allow yourself to disappear,
everything around you remains,
and also the one before you.

The other becomes even more present
when we disappear,
and it becomes easier to experience
the other not only as a body,
but as a being,
a consciousness
and one who sees us.

I invite you, then, to perceive the other
not only as an object,
but as an existence,
a "you."

When nothing is done, time can come to a halt, and space seems
to widen.

The more we stop doing, loving, and thinking, the more possible it
becomes that, forgetting our everyday identity, we become ourselves as space, which has no limits.

The quieter we are, the more we feel we live in an infinite universe.

And the greater our intuition of infinity, the more we can afford to
disappear.

6

Meeting Pain With Joy

We will make a different Vipassana today. I have spoken of Dukkha as an experience of feeling bad despite the apparent satisfactions of life; a deep dissatisfaction that we can discover in ourselves when we become more conscious—that is, less superficial. Especially for people of a cheerful nature, the process of entering into themselves—that is, in their deep reality—may not be so enjoyable.

When a therapeutic or spiritual process is undertaken, happiness is surely sought, but sometimes what happens can be likened to a descent into hell. Therapy leads to a greater awareness of internal conflicts and repressed emotions, and it is often painful to shed the idealized image of oneself and perceive the distance between one's own reality and one's own feelings.

In meditation the unsatisfactoriness of our life and our way of being is present, and we must learn to coexist with such dissatisfaction. Therefore, one way of meditating is precisely that of intensifying the discomfort. Pay attention to the discomfort and then learn to be before it with a good mood.

For although life is painful, nothing prevents us from smiling, and although the first of the Noble Truths is that which invites us to recognize the omnipresence of suffering, the images of the Buddha demonstrate smiling for us. It is fitting that we take this smile of his as an inspiration to help us smile even when life hurts.

In other words, however much suffering is sometimes inevitable, we are not doomed to be depressed. We can, alternatively, maintain in ourselves a positive attitude.

It is one of the teachings of Theravada Buddhism that joy is favorable to enlightenment, and we must recognize that joy exists on a plane other than suffering.

Ancient Buddhism recognizes a number of factors favorable to enlightenment, and one among them is the desire to know and understand, expressed in that spirit of inquiry that makes us "seekers of truth." Sometimes this desire for knowledge may seem like simple curiosity, but in meditative experience it leads us to truly want to know what we feel and even what we are. Or even "what it is." It is a kind of search for clarity that brings us to clarity.

Just as the desire to know becomes clarity, so it is with joy, which is a gift that we can cultivate in such a way that brings us to a type of satisfaction that does not depend on the satisfaction of our desires, but on our attitude towards the world.

For it is not the same to want to reject what hurts or bothers us, or to welcome it in a smiling way; or, more precisely, to welcome it without allowing us to remove the smile that is intrinsic to a loving attitude towards life and ourselves.

Today, I will invite you first to pay attention to the unsatisfactory aspect of the experience of the present, and then hold that attention with equanimity and finally with a smiling, cheerful, and kind attitude. But above all, to get together with someone you would like to know better.

We begin, as always, letting ourselves be as we are, without seeking or doing anything else.

Then we include our breathing in our field of consciousness.

And I invite you now to give some name to the feeling of this moment.

Peace? Indifference?
Irritation?
Craving?
The pleasure of rest?
A cheerful expectation?

If meditating is feeling the present, I invite you to especially feel
the emotional aspect of the present.

When we realize what we feel, it often happens that what we feel
changes more quickly. The more in contact we are with our emotional reality, the more it is transformed, like a stream of water that
crosses different landscapes. We are then open to the transformation of our feeling, which sometimes becomes more serene as we
meditate, but can also become more intense when we enter further
into it.

Just as our body has many parts and we can choose where we put
our attention, and just as we can attend to various aspects of our
sound environment, our emotional world is complex too, and we
can give preferential attention to the pleasure of the moment,
through greater surrender to rest and breathing.

And we can also pay special attention to our discomfort, our dissatisfaction. As much to our physical discomfort and the pain in our
legs as to our emotional discomfort and the existential suffering of
feeling far from the spiritual development to which we aspire,
capable of little love or understanding, too enslaved by our
passions...

Instead of avoiding what bothers us, we observe it directly, just
as when we have received a blow, we want to touch the wounded
area or as a dog licks its wounds—implicitly feeling that giving the
wounds attention helps to heal them.

I invite you to take direct knowledge of your own suffering, dissatisfaction or discomfort—with each breath.

But in Vipassana it is not simply a question of becoming aware of our experiences, as in psychotherapy; it is also a question of cultivating a balanced attitude, which is a detached, imperturbable consciousness.

But how to become imperturbable?

Only by becoming permeable, open to everything, without preferences, neutral.

As if the mind were a mirror that does not identify with the things it reflects. The mirror remains unchanged although what it is reflecting is a traumatic memory, or a tragic situation.

With each breath we attend to what in us is problematic, or incomplete, or unsatisfactory, but at the same time we try to look at it from a different point of view than the usual, everyday, and human view. Let us try to adopt the point of view of the mirror, which remains unchanged before what it reflects. Imagine that everything that happens in us is of a nature comparable to what is reflected in a mirror, and that we ourselves (that is, our consciousness) are like a mirror, which is as nothing, or as pure neutrality, pure receptivity.

We will now begin to open our eyes, always paying attention so as not to interrupt our inner state nor our practice of feeling the pain of the moment from the point of view of the imperturbability of a deep zone of our mind that is like a mirror that perceives everything and rejects nothing but remains unchanged in its emptiness.

Is it possible at this moment, despite the discomfort, the dissatisfaction, the emotional suffering and even the spiritual frustration, to have a greater acceptance? If we do not fight against what we dislike, but open ourselves to it without altering ourselves, can we perhaps smile a little at our problematic situation or our imperfections?

And if we can let everything be as it is, can we not adopt a kinder attitude, both towards ourselves and others?

Buddha formulated the truth of suffering,
but with a compassionate smile.
We can smile if we have found the deep peace
that lies deep in our minds,
because feeling our mind's depth is more fulfilling than the satisfaction of transient desires.
And even though life presents us with painful situations, doesn't smiling make them better?
And is our attitude toward pain not the main difference between neurosis and health?

We can suffer with irritation or suffer with some smiling imperturbability, with some equanimity. Upekkha.

We look up slowly to feel how it is different to look at the chest, neck, or mouth.

Without thought, we can observe how the experience of the other is modified, and then we prepare ourselves to meet through the gaze in an open attitude, without hiding the experience of the present, and without masking the face itself, allowing the other to perceive how we are, with all the deficiency that the moment may contain, all the discomfort, the imperfection of the moment, and if possible, also with acceptance.

We try to make our mind like an open space, transparent to what happens. And if we succeed, we will feel that this space that

welcomes everything in its neutrality makes us feel very good—
even though in our body and in our mind there are things that
may take a long time to digest.

7

Meditation in Pairs as a
Portal to Universal Compassion

We will start by letting ourselves be as we are ...
allowing us the experience and the attitude of the moment.
We do it with a loving attitude towards ourselves.
An attitude of friendship towards ourselves.

I invite you now to make a desire for happiness about yourself.
It should be easy to desire happiness, for is it not a universal desire,
that we all share?

But you may find obstacles to this proposal that I am advising.
Maybe they feel unfair, or undeserved, or perhaps there is in some
of you the will to punish yourself.
Be that as it may, I propose that you take it as a job and exercise in
yourself this small but important act of love for yourself.

Say to yourselves, "May I heal and flourish."
Or alternatively: "May I attain the fullness of spiritual maturity."
Observe the possible resistance that is made manifest when
you say it or want it, and insist on this act of friendship towards
yourselves.

And now try to desire a more earthly happiness: "May I have a happy life." Or: "May I find more satisfaction than suffering in love, in work, and in relationships with those around me."

Is it easier to desire worldly happiness or spiritual happiness? What objections do I harbor about happiness in my life?

Now I invite you to continue to hold open this aspiration to your own happiness.

You will surely feel selfish in the eyes of the other when you want happiness. I urge you, however, to allow this, and hold this act of love for yourself: "May I become happy both here on earth and in the heaven of spiritual fulfillment."

Only now do I invite you to include the other, making a wish for happiness for both of you. It will be something like, "God bless us" or "may grace fall upon us."

It is sometimes easier to desire good things for oneself than others, and sometimes the opposite, according to one's character.

But let us now take a step forward, including in our intention the group gathered here—only without distracting us from the person we have at the forefront, nor from ourselves. We want all of us to progress spiritually, heal, and be happy.

And now we go even further, trying to include in our benevolent intention even people with whom we have difficulties, with whom we are angry, or who irritate us.

Sometimes our desire to wish them well is not enough to achieve it but perhaps we can at least hope to forgive them someday and say to ourselves: "May I become so benevolent as to overcome this resentment."

Now imagine the unknown people who are in the space of the horizon. It is a very broad space, in which there will be many people more or less like ourselves, because humans have much in common, and we all suffer.

Let us observe how far we can extend our benevolence to them, and if we discover that we prefer not to desire happiness or psychospiritual progress, let us note our resistance and our objections.

Since our kindness and compassion are limited, we should develop them, so I recommend you take this opportunity to go beyond your own resistance, indifference, or misanthropy.

For this we can rely on music, because there is music that could not have been conceived without love and sometimes leads us to intuit what divine compassion could be.

Always including ourselves ("that I may fulfill my aspirations," "that I may cease to suffer"), the person whom we see before us, those who fill this room, and also many strangers around the place where we are.

But now we jump to a space much more than that of this region— the space of the whole country in which we are. It is almost impossible to imagine such a space, or to evoke the suffering of the people who occupy it, but if we want the great mass of strangers among those who live to be happy similarly to ourselves, this benevolent will transforms us. Or, rather, we discover a part of our nature we had not yet recognized.

And this will serve as a preparation for an even greater leap: To imagine the immensity of the planet we live in, with its billions of inhabitants, and how much suffering there is in this immense world, and to conceive a good will towards all beings, radiating benevolence that can embrace and benefit them.

And let us now take a much greater step, imagining that in the unlimited universe of multiple galaxies in which we find ourselves, we are not the only living or conscious beings, so that we can formulate the intention that all beings be blessed in each of the directions of inconceivable space—thus bringing our loving will to the intuition of the infinite.

2

A Minimal Introduction to Zazen

1

Non-Doing in the Context of Surrender and Generosity

I have mentioned that what is usually called Vipassana includes many variants of mindfulness, in which the focus may be on the body, on the emotions (or the motivational level of the experience), on thoughts, or on consciousness itself. In Zen, by contrast, the practice is more monolithic: non-doing, understood as sitting in silence and immobility.

It is true that many explanations about Zen meditation (Zazen) may be given, and teachers often provide them at the beginning of group sessions, but these relate more to the understanding achieved through the practice of non-doing, or constitute supplementary recommendations to the basic instruction of just sitting.

For now, in our first session together, I will only suggest that we at least focus on a different part of our body than in Vipassana, so that—instead of attending to the epigastrium or solar plexus—we focus on the *Hara*, a couple of finger-widths below the navel and slightly behind the abdominal wall. Through the practice of attending to this area, it is sometimes possible to feel something like an egg that the Taoist tradition calls the lower Dan-tien. It is enough that while practicing the stillness of "doing nothing but breathing" we shift our attention to our lower abdomen—which also evokes the feeling that our center of gravity is in the lower part of our body.

The practice of focusing on the *Hara* came into Zen fairly late, through the eighteenth century Japanese master Hakuin, who left us an autobiographical story of how he suffered from "Zen disease" (something equivalent to the dark night of the soul of Christian mystics) and was healed by a Taoist sage who transmitted the knowledge of the "circulation of the elixir"—in which the focus on the lower abdomen is an important aspect. Even though the practice of focusing on the *Hara* persisted in Zen while the rest of the Taoist inner alchemy did not, its importance is universally recognized, and it is understood not just as placing one's attention in the lower abdomen, but something like a "thinking downward"—a letting oneself sink into one's pelvis while surrendering to gravity, as if one's whole body might want to sink into the earth.

This will be enough for our present session in regard to sitting properly. But now I want to say something about the gesture of reverence we engage in as we bow with our palms together in front of our heart. The meaning of this gesture at the beginning of a meditation session is different than at the end, for at the beginning we feel that we make ourselves small in front of something bigger or of greater import (Buddhahood or the mystery of the Enlightened Mind) that we hope we may come to know—and before which the best we can presently do is surrender. By becoming small in face before the infinite, we want to disappear before the Supreme Reality, which is to say that—if we get ourselves out of the way—it may be that such surrender is sufficient for the Wisdom Mind to swallow us, turning us into its own transcendent body.

After meditation, however, the same gesture constitutes a ritual act different from that of surrendering. Now it entails an act of giving, and more specifically one of giving away or offering the merit we may have gained through our meditation session. For, just as we endeavor to dissolve in the ocean of universal consciousness, it behooves us to cultivate generosity, which is the reverse of the temptation to hoard the outcome of our practice.

This is the practice of "offering the merit," in which we may take a very simple act of bowing to mean that, instead of adding the (unknown) merit of our last sitting to that already accumulated in our seeker's "enlightenment curriculum," we make it available, instead, to those in need, or to divine beings or Buddhas dwelling in the different directions of galactic space, who will know how to best distribute our "grain of sand" (along with the contributions of others) to our common benefit.

It makes sense to offer our spiritual work not only at the end of a session but also, of course, at any time, since it behooves us to make Bodhichitta—dedication to the path of enlightenment as a service to all—the background of all our practices in daily life.

2

From "Not Even Non-doing" (Wu Wu Wei) to the Realization That "From the Beginning Nothing Existed"

Just as the Jewish tradition speaks of three patriarchs, Abraham, Isaac and Jacob (while Joseph does not receive the same designation), the history of Zen calls only the first six great masters "patriarchs." I cannot say that I can explain why after the sixth patriarch there is no mention of a seventh or an eighth. Did the disciples of the Sixth Patriarch feel that no one in his generation could measure up to the depth of Hui Neng, and so he came to be considered the last of the patriarchs? In any case, I think that an introduction to Zen meditation should include some elements of Zen culture, and thus some of the history of what followed the arrival in China of the mysterious Bodhidharma, the First Patriarch, who apparently traveled from the same region of ancient "India" as Padmasambhava—though little is known about him besides the fact that for many years he meditated facing the wall of a Shaolin temple without being noticed. After being recognized as a great master, he came to be interrogated by the Emperor, who was not satisfied by his answers (particularly when, to the question concerning what merit his actions had in favor of Buddhism, Bodhidharma is said to have answered: "No merit whatsoever").

After Bodhidharma, there is nobody more important to know about than the sixth and last Patriarch, Hui Neng (or Wei Lang), whose formulation of Zen left an indelible mark on the future of Zen in China, Korea, Japan, and the world.

Hui Neng himself has recounted how, having lost his father as a child, he supported his mother by collecting firewood. One day, as he was going about his business, he heard someone singing something that touched him deeply. He inquired about the words of that song, and was told it was the Diamond Sutra, which was chanted in a certain monastery, and this was enough for him to seek it and present himself at its gate. There he was interrogated by the abbot—the Fifth Patriarch—who asked him where he came from and the boy, not feeling intimidated, answered something to the tenor of, "what does it matter where one comes from?" The master, recognizing the boy's potential, put him to work in the kitchen, washing rice.

The story continues and it is explained that several years later the abbot summoned a contest to determine which of his disciples, having reached a deeper understanding of his teachings, should be his successor. The wall of a gallery had been cleaned so that the applicants could write, and the most respected one among the disciples had written and posted a poem there that was being repeated by everyone. When the news reached the boy who pounded rice in the kitchen, he asked a monk to take him to the site and read him the poem, since he could not read. That poem, which has now become famous, stated:

The body is like the tree of enlightenment,
the mind, a shining mirror.
You must clean this mirror
so that it does not gather dust.

Upon hearing this, the young Hui-Neng asked the monk if he would write something for him, and then dictated another set of lines, which have become even more famous than those of the Fifth Patriarch's model disciple.

Neither is awakening like a tree
nor does a mirror shine anywhere.
Since from the beginning nothing has existed,
where might the dust settle?

Later, two contrasting methods came to be followed in the Zen world: one according to which meditation was a removal of the dust obscuring the mind's mirror so that it can reflect reality; the other, more mysterious, sought the essence of Zen through insight into the illusoriness of all phenomena.

The story of Hui Neng continues with his secret visit to his master's room where, under cover of darkness, the Patriarch recognized him as his successor and gave him his robe and his bowl as symbols of his transmission. Realizing that this nomination would not be acceptable to the rest of the disciples, however, he advised him to flee the monastery before dawn.

The story ends when one of the monks in pursuit caught up with Hui Neng and explained that they did not want to take away his robe, but only sought enlightenment. To this, Hui Neng responded: "Without thinking anything good or bad, how was your original face before your parents were born?" I suppose that this act of transmission had results, for Hui Neng's question about the "original face" has remained in the annals of Zen as one of the Koans, or topics of meditation, used in the tradition for both training and for the examination of disciples' understanding.

Apparently, Hui Neng and his rival, the model disciple, taught during the same period (one in the North and the other in the South, each one with his distinctive method). Yet history would prove that the way of understanding that "from the beginning nothing existed" has been the most fruitful.

Yet how can simple "non-doing" lead to the seemingly amazing and rare realization that "from the beginning nothing has ever existed"? I hope I can convey some notion of it in the course of this series of sessions, but for now let me just say that the first step towards it is a degree of non-doing that may lead us beyond thought, to the empty nature of our deeper mind.

Let us, then, place our attention for now on the breath in the *Hara*, and practice once more "not even non-doing."

This time, I invite you to adopt the distinctive Zazen hand position, which is similar to that of the Theravada meditation tradition but somewhat more precise, since you not only place the back of one hand into the palm of the other but you curve your hands as if forming a bowl and close the ellipse thus formed with the thumbs meeting above.

Through this ritual gesture, one feels not only centered, but as if one holds in one's hands a precious treasure. (Also, significantly, an empty one).

Furthermore, since this is a gesture traditionally associated with the Buddha himself, the mere fact of adopting it implies that we are imitating the Buddha.

Just as in the Christian faith, the "imitation of Christ" is a way of approaching the ideal, this hand position gives an implicitly devotional aspect to the act of meditation, through which the meditator feels invited to expect that as he divests himself of thought, he will be identifying with the Buddhahood within him—his true nature.

In addition to its reference to the Buddha of iconography and legend, the hand position described naturally leads one's attention to the hands, and not just towards the belly and our center. This in turn, along with Hara awareness, entails some measure of consciousness of the whole body—in spite of the instruction to "drop" the body, which exists in our thinking mind, so as to be fully interested in the subject of consciousness itself.

Finally, it is known in monasteries (where practice extends for long periods) how the precise position of the thumbs requires an alert mind that is difficult to maintain when there is drowsiness.

Hence, in places where the instructor uses a rod to hit the back of the meditators to recapture their attention, it is the position of the thumbs that sometimes inspires this correction.

I will not say more for now, since it should be more than enough to indicate that the practice of not-doing may bring us to a point where effort is no longer involved, a state of restful ease where meditation is no longer a psychological exercise but a state of "not even non-doing."

NOT EVEN NOT-DOING

This time for a change, we will have a silent session until we open our eyes.

Now, as you open your eyes, I invite you to observe the possible discontinuity of your attention, surely fatigued.

Every time you realize that you have been distracted by your thoughts, simply return to the stillness of non-doing.

And now let us continue doing the same while raising our gaze until we meet face to face,
which allows for the contagion of attention
and a contagion of self-abandonment;

For when meditation reaches a certain depth,
it becomes contagious,
and even self-forgetfulness can inspire a witness to "disappear."

When focus is sufficient,
there remains only breath,
breathing without an "I."

3

What Are Your Thoughts Up To?

During moments of grace, we can spontaneously do nothing or spontaneously surrender ourselves to restfulness by simply dropping onto our seats and into our pelvis; then the breath becomes present and relaxation of the mind follows relaxation of the body.

But sometimes non-doing becomes a task, as does paying attention and focusing on the Hara. Even remembering this triple task of non-doing, letting oneself sink toward the floor, and focusing on the Hara may not be so easy. Our thoughts may be so distracting that we even forget our purpose.

What can we do, then?
Perhaps nothing, other than accepting that this is a difficult day, and generating as much attention as we can.

As you open your eyes this time, I invite you to pay particular attention to the periphery of your visual field, and you will see that this way of looking, less practical than the usual way, is more consistent with the open and free attitude of meditation.

It is as if we are looking in all directions at once.

I invite you once again to look up slowly, until you meet face-to-face, only this time, looking more towards the periphery of the visual field than to a certain point.

Facing one another, look at space rather than focusing on each other's faces.

And now observe what you do while not intending to do anything.
What is so compulsive that you cannot stop doing it?
And if you find yourself thinking, what are your thoughts about?
What are you looking for through your thinking?
What do your thoughts want from you?

Did this inquiry help us to let go of some useless thinking?

Now we'll take a few minutes to share briefly about the experience of silent face to face meditation, and to say goodbye.

4

Shikantaza

Legend says that for many years, Bodhidharma—the First Patriarch of Ch'an—meditated facing a wall in a Shao Lin temple and nobody took interest in him until Huike, who later would succeed him as the Second Patriarch, waited a long time for the opportunity to get his attention. It is said that Huike stood in the snow until it reached his knees and then, stepping forward, cut his arm with his sword as a sacrifice and as proof of his sincerity in asking for his teaching.

It is said that the master, Bodhidharma, with no drama whatsoever asked him, "What do you want?" He answered, "My soul is tortured," and the master replied, "Show me your soul."

When the seeker said he could not find it, the teacher said, "I have already cleaned it for you."

It is said that, in this moment, Huike attained enlightenment. But how can you understand this exchange, which in no way involved a simple verbal dialogue?

Not finding your own soul amounts, naturally, to the discovery of the truth of non-self, which in turn is the universal experience of Buddhist meditation. Not finding the soul (that Mahayana, as we have seen, formulates as finding emptiness) is nothing but enlightenment. But it seems that it is precisely ceasing to find within us something visible or describable that transforms the "not finding anything" into a "finding nothing"—which is finding the mystery.

Naturally, it is not something logical, and we know that it is something that happens instantly, in a given moment—even if it involves not only the focus of meditation, but surely all of life and its merits.

One aspect of meditation, then, is to focus no longer on "things," but on focus itself—i.e., on the invisible presence of the subject of consciousness, which is something like nothing.

But this practice requires something like being used to having an empty mind, which, in view of our oral disposition (which is always looking for something new to eat or suck), involves frustration, and it can be a long time before we manage to be satisfied with stillness.

The practice I want to introduce today is called Shikantaza—a word that is sometimes translated as "only sitting." The "za" means "sit," "shikan" translates as "nothing but" and the syllable "ta" between the two (shikan-ta-za) indicates emphasis, making the term as a whole mean something like, "to sit strenuously." That is, just be there, but with the determination and intense focus of a samurai who could be killed by the sword of an opponent if he becomes distracted.

In short, it is an attitude towards our own thoughts, comparable to that of a warrior for whom the distraction from his task can be a matter of life and death. Such attention is fierce for its determination (as expressed in the eyes of Bodhidharma, that we may see

through his portraits and caricatures) to sustain non-doing without
the distraction of thoughts. Paradoxically, however, Wu wei is not
only stillness, but also allowing the mind's spontaneous activity,
and may permit a meditation that is not distracted from inner
silence even in the midst of thoughts.

But let us practice now, always with our focus on the continuity of
breath and the Hara.

Let's continue now with eyes open, as it is done in the classic
Shikantaza.

Naturally, for a beginner the focus will be intermittent, particularly
because the practice is fatiguing and focus is susceptible to fatigue.
But every time we become distracted we return to nothing as one
returns home.

Let's now move on to meeting with open eyes, to allow the possibility of a transfer of energy or focus, because when you truly
accomplish meditation, it is naturally contagious, and with good
concentration all we have left is breath—ideally breath without
even a self.

5

Dropping the Body and the Mind

One might think that simply non-doing is enough to become nothing, and thus join all. But meditation is not everything, and in the Buddhist context it is proposed that meditation should be linked to virtuosity—that is, an ethical way of life.

As in the Judeo-Christian culture, doing the least possible damage, avoiding lying, and avoiding greed are considered an essential part of the path. It is also considered part of the path to *understand* certain things, to understand "the teachings." And it is understanding that is considered the most important.

When it comes to enlightenment, it is not so much about altered states of consciousness, but about a vivid understanding of such things as the Four Noble Truths, which explain not only the origin of our suffering in ignorance and attachment, but also the path to liberation and wisdom.

But although understanding is not something purely rational but also experiential, this is expressed differently in the ancient and Mahayana traditions. One difference, as explained, refers to the supreme state. In ancient Buddhism, it is highlighted that you must go from Samsara—which is running in circles and therefore a prison, also compared to a sea in which we drown—to Nirvana, which is like "the other shore" of salvation (and an annihilation of the ordinary mind). However, in Mahayana it is recognized that the emptiness of Nirvana is not something separate from Samsara, but its ubiquitous foundation. Thus, as the Heart Sutra says, "emptiness is form and form is emptiness." But is the notion that the divine underlies all things and all beings not something also typical of Western mysticism?

Surely the significance of the apparent duality between the divine and the world, and even between the sacred and the profane, is known in all spiritual traditions but the more the spiritual experiences are coated with popular religious phenomena—social, patriarchal phenomena linked to competition and striving for supremacy—the more these differences in languages become apparent, rather than the similarity of the experiences that have inspired them.

Make no mistake, then, to think that different concepts necessarily refer to different visions, and that the aspiration to Nirvana is of a different nature than the aspiration to the Kingdom of Heaven, even though in both East and West the novice's view differs from the mature vision of those who have understood the supreme unity of the transcendent and the world.

I think the most eloquent way it has been explained was by the Vedic tradition, long before Buddhism: that the whole (which is one), as it becomes the universe, is fragmented like a tree that a divine lumberjack has destroyed by splitting it in pieces. This divine sacrifice of the All that is dismembered in Creation is seen as symmetrical to the sacrifice of fire that, as it burns wood and all kinds of objects (and animals, and perhaps even people), returns the parts of the multiplicity to the All, the visible to the invisible, and the personal self to the One.

I like this image of the visible world as a tree with an invisible root that is like the underlying unity of the many branches of its foliage, particularly because we know that—apart from the contrast between its visibility / invisibility—root and crown are similar. I think this concept is perfectly consistent with the vision of things proposed by David Bohm, an Einstein collaborator, who contrasted the "implicit order" of the universe with the "explicit order" of the visible universe.

It is as if the intuition of the unity of things was present in the human mind and although we live in the conceptual and practical mind that only perceives multiplicity, another, wiser, part of our mind can (when our practice and instrumental mind becomes still and silent) understand the communion of all in nothingness.

This union or non-multiplicity is described in Mahayana Buddhism not only as a non-self, but as emptiness—Shunyata in Sanskrit. But how can we reach this vacuum of which nothing can be said, for it has no characteristics that can identify it? Through a "dis-identification" with all things in the world of multiplicity.

And that is something we can achieve simply through the attitude of dropping the world—as long as we are disappointed and tired enough of our eager attachment.

And this is the formula that I want to invite you to apply today: *let everything drop.*

"Dropping all" may be a more precise instruction than "disidentifying" from all, isolating or renouncing oneself—even if it is also its equivalent. For though the process of spiritual development in all spiritual traditions implies renunciation, when one speaks of "dropping," one is speaking of a less theoretical language and closer to the experience of stillness. It indicates, first of all, a dropping of the body, which is like surrendering to gravity, letting yourself fall to the ground.

When we drop to the ground, we not only feel like our whole sitting body rests on the pelvis, but we feel like a mountain.

If in normal life we feel as if we live behind our eyes, letting ourselves drop shifts our center of gravity to the *Hara*, inviting us to feel as if we live in our lower abdomen.

While returning from Japan a few years ago, I found that in a kiosk at the airport they sold a doll with the face of the well-known first Patriarch of Zen that could not be knocked down, as his center of gravity was near the base. It was one of those dolls that always remains vertical, which I found very evocative of the spirit of Zazen, done with the spine erect but whose experiential secret is to let oneself drop on the *Hara*—and on the earth.

Legend has it that Bodhidharma had set out to not fall asleep during meditation with such determination that, upon failing in his efforts, one day he cut his eyelids so he could no longer shut them. When I used to see Fritz Perls, it seemed to me that his look was similar to that of Bodhidharma, so it was hard for me to be with him. Just having him in front of me during some of our meals was subtly frightening and because his presence was so intense, I could not lie while around him—but everything you said turned into a lie in his presence.

I was saying that a first aspect of "dropping everything" is to drop the body—i.e., surrender it to its natural weight and to the earth— which leads to feeling that the center of gravity is in the abdomen, but it is also important, of course, to drop the thoughts that fill our mind.

Dropping the body predisposes us to drop our everyday mind, with its thoughts and tasks, but that is not enough for it to happen. Therefore, we should also intend to drop the mind, with which we identify, and therefore we feel that dropping it is something like disappearing or dying.

We could say that we have enough for today with this double formula of dropping the body and the mind. But if someone wanted to go further, he could observe what remains after one has dropped the body as much as the thoughts, the emotions, and the desires.

Conceptually, we can say that there is nothing left. But when we convert the question into experiential research, we might find something more subtle than thought and other mental phenomena: a pure consciousness, which is usually invisible to itself.

It is precisely the purpose of Zen meditation to discover this fundamental consciousness beyond mental phenomena. That is what is called satori or kensho, which means awakening.

But rushing to find it now would not only be proceeding with undue haste, but in the wrong direction, because to find what is not of this world, we must first rid ourselves of all haste and even the spirit of seeking.

6

The Subtle Attention of Nirvana

We drop our body to earth and observe the upright position of our spine without any effort.
It just requires a small amount of attention to find a balanced position, in which each vertebra of our spine rests on the one below it, using minimum effort.

We drop the body, but keep the focus on the breath.
Although we lose interest in everything, we continue paying attention to the breath.

We also drop the mind.

"Dropping the mind" is something different from "combatting our thoughts." Just as when we go to sleep at night, in meditation we lose interest not only in the external world, but also the inner world, with its thoughts, desires, and emotions—
that is, our psychological world.

If we manage to drop it all we become empty.

This is why Zazen is described sometimes as a state of no-mind
But unfamiliarity with this empty state makes it difficult for us to
linger there.
Only for brief moments, that we must renew, can we accomplish it.
This is a good way to practice,
and thus cultivate a calm and quiet mind,
with no desires and no irritation,
and maybe thus achieve not doing anything more easily than
through the most obvious and direct formula of "non-doing."

Of course, even when we drop the world, when we open our eyes
we see what lies in front of us, in the same manner as you are still
listening to my voice.

But this doesn't mean that while "letting it all drop" nothing has
happened. It is as if the field of focus has opened.
Although we see, we see without looking,
not looking for anything,
just letting the visual world
penetrate us.
Then we start looking up very slowly, toward the face-to-face
encounter,
always trying to just breathe,
sustaining the non-doing,
just dropping the body into the ground with no intention, including the intention of finding a different state of consciousness ...

In an attempt to convey in a nutshell something about Zen, I said
something seemingly contradictory: I said that meditation involves
a search for the absolute—which is something very big that sur-
passes rational understanding—and that the path of the search for
self leads to the discovery of Buddhahood, which is consciousness
itself. But for one who has not come to live the awakening of enlightenment, consciousness does not seem like anything special (unlike
the objects of consciousness, which can be).

Consciousness may even seem boring if it is not associated with something extraordinary, and in the ordinary condition of mind, consciousness is always associated with something; Western philosophy does not recognize that it can be otherwise.

It is said that consciousness must always be awareness of something (which results in the claim that consciousness is "intentional") and it is inconceivable that the subject of consciousness may have an existence independent of its objects.

It is seemingly contradictory, then, that we seek something big that lies within us as a precious treasure, while on the other hand we are advised to understand that the consciousness that we seek is something very ordinary and we better shed any expectation of anything extraordinary.

Already in the idea of emptiness we find this paradox that what seems like nothing is the basis of everything.

Simple reasoning already allows us to understand that our whole perception of the world is seated in consciousness, and therefore there would be no world without consciousness. Only that, in Buddhism, there is the expectation of a phenomenological or experiential understanding that consciousness is like the raw material of which all things are made, hence it is claimed that all forms are manifestations of emptiness. But how can the tangible world be formed of a raw material that cannot even (according to Mahayana) be said to exist?

I am not speaking now of philosophy, but of the spirit of meditation, approached with the aspiration of something larger and deeper than ourselves that also requires being satisfied with finding nothing or, as has been said, left empty handed and going nowhere.

Because meditation is an invitation to discount our egoic or passionate motivations, it is an education in neutrality, which renounces any excess. But because meditation is a path to wisdom and other virtues, we can say that through non-doing we enrich ourselves. Only we must understand that in non-doing we must give up the search itself.

But is this not similar to Christianity, in which it is said that one must surrender to receive grace, or be willing to give one's life to save the soul or die to be reborn? Only when one looks inside and finds nothing is it recommended to observe this nothing. After dropping the body and dropping the mind, when there is nothing, meditation consists of looking at this nothing.

But one has to learn to look without the hope of finding something great, because this hope keeps us from true receptivity, which is like seeing without looking, or seeing without searching.

We must familiarize ourselves with our quiet mind, focusing on our own attention with a detachment that is unlike our usual hunter mentality. We are too barbarous and eager for the mystery of the deep mind, unless we develop the subtle focus of Nirvana.

7

The Truth That Can Set Us Free

Surely it has become evident that the mind becomes more silent while non-doing, but to some extent the individual also becomes nothing.

Furthermore, when you reach sufficient experience with the stilling of thought, you get to understand that the ordinary world is sustained by thought, and that even our body exists in thought.

The entire universe is dependent on our conceptual mind, which names things and identifies our sensory impressions. But when we become familiar with the inner silence that underlies our perception of everything, it is possible that we may gradually identify more with that empty core than with the multiplicity of mental phenomena. As such, what was simply a central void in us comes to be lived not only as the basis of our mind, but as the *basis of everything.*

Surely this feeling (and not just thinking or believing) that everything is sustained by consciousness itself (which of course does not belong to us) is an experience that has been known outside Buddhism. Thus we read, in Idries Shah's book on Rumi, an anecdote about a saint who, at the end of his forty days of fasting, met Maulana, who was absorbed in his mind "in the nowhere in the heights" and commented:

"What is in the world is nothing but what is in you." Adding then, as a corollary to this: "Seek in yourself all you want, for you are everything."

Gaining access to the empty mind, then, is like gaining access to a universal raw material—a consciousness of which all things are made, as has been proposed by the idealistic philosophies, in spite of its unpopularity in the contemporary scientific world.

In Zen this mind behind all is referred to as the "original face" according to the famous Koan of Hui Neng, which asks, "How was your original face before your parents were born?"

The so-called Koans emerged in the Zen tradition as teacher's formulations that were later collected as enigmas, the answers to which must be sought through meditation, and teachers have used them to test their disciples. This is one of the most famous. But how can it be understood?

It refers, of course, to our fundamental identity, which is not physical or even individual but cosmic and that is discovered when one who has already been stripped of his vanity and his illusions discovers that his small day-to-day mind is but an island in the ocean of infinite mind, which is our common, deep, and true identity.

The process of the development of consciousness does not end with the experience of the great empty and self-aware mind which is called Buddhahood (much as in Western mysticism the path does not end with the experience of the divine) but evolves into the integration of spiritual awareness into life, and the perception of the divine in all things.

One of the most quoted statements of Mahayana Buddhism that is recited every day in Zen monasteries (because it is part of the brief Heart Sutra) refers precisely to this: "Form is emptiness and emptiness is form."

To say that form is emptiness is like saying that the visible universe is like an iceberg in which the hidden part is the largest; it is also equivalent to the distinction between a manifested world and an unmanifested world.

But it is not so easy to reach the deeper reality through meditation, and the difficulty is explained in the Zen tradition through the story of a princess—Enyadatta—who discovers one day that she has no head.

Everyone has a head on their upper body, but one day Enyadatta discovers she cannot see hers, and worries about being different from other mortals. Thus, after discovering she has no head, the princess begins to scream desperately, running from one place to another looking for it, until, to protect her from her own madness, they tie her to one of the columns in the palace. Though unable to move, she is still in great agitation and—while trying desperately to move—hits her head against the column. She then shouts: "Finally! I found my head!"

Only after we begin to look within and fail to find the soul, or the self we thought we had, do we begin to seek it, without knowing yet that this soul or mind that we are searching for (that is not of this world) cannot be seen nor heard nor even singled out in terms of any characteristics or conceptual features—although it can be perceived through another form of cognition, which Buddhism calls Wisdom and Christianity calls Truth (as in "truth will set you free"): a spiritual perception in which consciousness reveals itself directly.

We could say that at the bottom of each one of us is what we sense as the divine or, more precisely, we may come to realize that *the light of our consciousness, with which we perceive all things, is in itself divine*.

Yet ordinary consciousness—which illuminates everything we want to see without making itself visible—is not something that we can perceive as divine. Our blindness to the sacredness of the light, with which we light up everything that we see, might be compared to what is said about fish: that they cannot see the water in which they are moving precisely because it is so familiar to them.

Nor is it different from what is explained in the Sufi tradition through one of the jokes attributed to the legendary Nasrudin, where we are told that he crossed a border over and over again with his donkey where the inspectors, convinced he was smuggling, would always check him carefully. They could never confirm their suspicion so, when they ran into him many years later, they asked him directly: "What were you smuggling when we could never catch you?" And the answer from the famous and witty Nasrudin was: "Donkeys."

The metaphor of the princess who could not find her own head until she hit herself means that even though it is true that the ordinary mind cannot access the spiritual reality, it makes sense to persist in seeking another form of cognition. This is what is called "researching the nature of mind."

But as I said, we should not think that this deep self-knowledge is something that has only been known in Buddhism. When it is said in the Christian tradition that "the truth will set us free," it is precisely that truth which has its foundation in itself. When the oracle of Apollo recommended to know thyself, surely he was also referring to this meeting with the core of self beyond our surface characteristics, social roles, and personality. Anyone who has known the work of Gurdjieff surely knows the main task toward which such work was headed: "self remembering." These words do not refer to the importance of recognizing one's own desires, as befits resigned and alienated people, but to regaining consciousness of a "fundamental mind" which we have all forgotten through our childhood development. For we are born ignorant of the world but, aware of what we have forgotten, strive to find it again. In the womb, we probably already participated in union with the whole and swam in that oceanic experience that, according to Freud, we want to recover through mysticism.

Learning so many things that demand our attention—which is forced learning in an authoritarian society—has led us to forget ourselves. Through meditation we want to regain contact with what we have always been but have come to ignore.

We will now begin the meditation; the suggestion that I will very briefly make is that when our minds quiet down, even though thoughts will still come through, try to identify more with the stillness than with the thoughts that come across.

It is a fact that we are at the intersection of two worlds—that of silence and that of perceptions and thoughts—but we can choose to identify more with the silent space of our mind than with the content that fills it.

There comes a time in the practice of meditation in which it is understood that mental phenomena (forms) sit in the empty mind, which is pure consciousness, similar to how the light of a projector is the underlying reality of the film projected in a theater. For this we must first learn to dis-identify with the film and its drama through a kind of cosmic immutability.

My invitation this time is to, imagining ourselves as an immutable ocean, let our oceanic nature open to the existence of algae, fish, and water currents. In other words: let us try to identify with emptiness while resisting the temptation to identify with ongoing mental events.

8

Renouncing the Objects of Consciousness to Return to Ourselves

Sometimes non-doing is enough for us to disappear.

But at other times it helps us to drop the body, dropping the center of gravity towards the abdomen.

And even more, to drop our ordinary mind, with all its contents.

Dropping the mind is something like invoking stillness, which is something similar to what gravity is for the body.

So we can overcome thinking to some extent.

But when our mind is quiet, empty of thoughts, we observe the empty mind.

What is there, where there is nothing?

There is the observer, surely. The subject of consciousness.

But usually we cannot observe the observer.

And when you look within yourself and nothing is found, it can be difficult to stay in this nothing.

For in our greed we want more than nothing, and do not resist the temptation to fill it with something.

Therefore, the first step is simply familiarizing ourselves with the invisibility of the subject of our consciousness—despite observing, we can't perceive what we observe.

Let's continue now with our eyes open.

Although our ordinary consciousness is one in which the subject always expects to find satisfaction in an object, in meditation we want to give up such hunger for objects. The masters tell us in their testimonials that someday the subject of our consciousness will find the supreme satisfaction when it finds itself.

The technique of panoramic view can be a useful detail because it induces an attitude of detachment that leads us to feel the center of ourselves.

Even though sometimes it is an effort to be interested in ourselves, it is also possible that the day comes when we find that nothing is as appealing as coming home and staying there.

9

The Ocean and the Waves

Although we have been talking about form and emptiness, the inspiring metaphor that I will suggest for this meditation is the ocean and its waves; that is, the contrast between the water and the shapes of the water's movement on its surface.

The image of a thinking mind as a lake on whose surface there are waves that prevent the landscape or the sun from being reflected is very old. This old analogy from the Yogi tradition has been modified by Mahayana, which makes its own equivalence between thought and the drawings formed by the movement of water on its surface but poses—as an achievement of the stilling of such thoughts or unrest—*the possibility of perceiving the water itself.*

Let us still, then, our mental activity, in order to perceive our mind itself without being distracted by its movement.

Can we know ourselves as "water" even when our mind moves? Can we keep our silence even when some thoughts are coming through?

Now let us continue with our eyes open.

Let us raise our sight, allowing the encounter between two minds that rest in their emptiness.

Finally, let us disappear while we pay special attention to the feeling that the other exists.

In other words, the other is not a thing in front of us, but a consciousness, a you.

10

About the Bodhisattva Ideal and the Virtue of Being Satisfied with Counting Breaths

I should say something more about the Bodhisattva ideal. As I have already explained, Arhat—a form of holiness in which the individual has given up passions—was the ideal of ancient Buddhism. But the Mahayana ideal—the Bodhisattva—is of a somewhat different kind of holiness which resembles Christian holiness for its emphasis on love.

I Imagine that the Buddhists who, in the early centuries, had mainly sought their individual salvation, realized gradually the contradiction between detachment and the ideal formulated in these terms, finding that in their anxiety to reach the other shore they had become somewhat selfish. Is it not possible that a man dedicated to his spiritual progress comes into conflict with his family? I remember reading a poem in Tagore's *Gitanjali*, in which a seeker tells God that he will leave everything to meet him and God responds through the eyes of his wife and her son: "I am here, stay."

The well-known Tibetan Lama Chogyam Trungpa used in the Seventies the term "spiritual materialism" in reference to the greed of spiritual progress which complicates the lives of seekers who lose sight of the understanding that, while on the path, the balance between wisdom and method matters; that is, the balance between meditation and the development of virtues, or between empathy and compassion.

The emphasis of Mahayana Buddhism on compassion is expressed by a reference to the Bodhisattvas' renunciation of Buddhahood and also the precept that states that we should devote ourselves to our spiritual progress not only for our own sake, but for the sake of everyone.

The so-called "Bodhisattva vow," through which the Mahayana follower is committed to work for the salvation of all, might sound crazy in our culture, where interest in the salvation of everyone tends to be considered a messianic attitude. It is especially schizophrenic or narcissistic people who speak of themselves as saviors. But in Buddhism it is well known that when one has reached sufficient personal progress, it is natural that one begins to care for others. It is also known in shamanism that he who has healed spontaneously begins "shamanizing," and even feels bad if not in the service of another's well-being. By this I mean that it is natural in human life to reach a time when it is no longer necessary to take care of oneself and one becomes more generous; throughout the history of Buddhism, this maturation process became a cultural tenet. Then, feeling that from a certain point on the road, being too concerned with ourselves could be compared to a spiritual hypochondria, some may have wanted to draw attention to the importance of not staying fixed in the pursuit of a purely individual salvation.

I remember reading about the meeting of Martin Buber with someone who reproached himself for having abandoned his prayers and for having stopped attending synagogue. Buber chided him for such admonishments, pointing out that when there was so much to do, it was better to occupy himself with serving instead of worrying so much about his own spirituality.

Sometimes whoever undertakes the inner journey is only interested in suffering less, but one who already understands his spiritual potential advances with a different motivation, and one who continues to advance also wants to become a person capable of helping others.

It is therefore recommended that from the beginning one fosters a real motivation to purify one's mind and awaken the transcendent mystery, not only for one's own benefit but to serve the evolution of others. And although the beginner has not yet discovered such motivation to serve—and therefore to acknowledge it might seem false—it is beneficial to anticipate the discovery that in reality we are not as selfish as we believe, and thus hasten our arrival to health, which makes us participants in the web of life as we discover we are "ecological beings" rather than isolated individuals. In addition, letting go of some of our insistence in reaching the light, as if it were a meritorious achievement, will prove to be an advantage as much as impatience is a disadvantage.

Suzuki Roshi (founder of the first Zen monastery in California) wanted to convey such a lack of hurry to get results when he said: "Sitting is so good. But it is also so good to walk. And it is so good, being able to *Gassho* (bowing in salutation) and then just sitting." Everything was an opportunity that he lived with gratitude and with no hurry.

It is clear, then, that the Bodhisattva condition is one in which our own spiritual thirst has been left behind and, as such, we can afford generosity, which is the first of the virtues that are suggested as steps on the "Bodhisattva path." As explained by Shantideva in his classic text on the subject, the ethical sense of life or purity, heroic energy, peace, and focusing ability will develop from generosity—and all these will in turn be needed as wisdom awakens. But for the seeker who has not yet realized that the gates of paradise do not open for those who arrive with claims or arguments about why they should be let in, surely paradise on earth will become a purgatory.

The meditation to which I invite you today is one that is widely practiced as part of the Zen training but comes across as much less interesting or profound than Shikantaza. It consists simply of counting breaths.

Each breathing cycle is assigned a number ranging from 1 to 10, either inhalation or exhalation, and when it reaches ten it is restarted.

Naturally, it is not difficult to count the breaths mechanically, but this may not have any effect on the development of our focus.

If I count my breaths intently, surely I will get it easily, but if I do it without thinking about anything, it may be difficult to reach ten, because in my inner silence I will lose count.

I will hesitate, for example, if six is next or seven. In that case I would have to begin again and it could happen that after half an hour I never reach ten.

If—instead of resolving to simply count breaths, which we may find of little significance—we count breaths in an attitude of non-doing or just being there (attending more to being present than accomplishing a task), it will not be less interesting.

Which reminds me of what Suzuki Roshi once said to Charlotte Selver, the woman who brought Sensory Awareness from Germany to the United States. After a few days of practice, she told him she already felt that he did it well. Suzuki's response was that he could stop counting and move on to the practice of "just breathing"—that is, Zazen.

It is curious that counting breaths constitutes a humbler exercise than not counting.

Not counting can sometimes be something like Alice's fall into the well of the unknown at the beginning of her adventure.

But counting is much more mundane because this detail keeps us on the surface of the mind, which requires greater humility and less verbalness; or, put another way, more verbal frustration.

But let's go now to the practice, and we will not do anything besides counting every exhalation from one to ten. Although this is a technique that is usually presented as a preliminary to Shikantaza, it is not a bad idea to appreciate it not only as an exercise in focusing, but also one in simplicity and especially acceptance of the simplicity of the now. Doing it well is part of mental wellness, that is, doing it without suffering from the deprivation of something more important.

11

Words of Dogen

Frequently when one begins to enter the practice of Zen, the teacher will give you the task of just counting breaths. It is also common to place much of your attention on posture right from the beginning of the practice of Zazen.

In what we have done during these days, however, I began by explaining the innermost and subtle aspects of the practice, and I believe this is consistent with the attitude of the old masters, who were more interested in the transmission of internal truths than in how to sit.

In the same spirit I will conclude this brief introduction to Zen with a quote from Dogen, a Japanese teacher who traveled to China and wrote a body of work—the Shobogenzo—as prestigious as that of the patriarchs, which could be considered the culmination of this spiritual current.

Knowing the path of awakening
Is to know yourself;
Knowing yourself
Is to forget yourself;

Forgetting yourself
Is to be enlightened by all things;
Being enlightened by all things
Is to let your body and mind disappear
From oneself and everything else;
Then the remnants
Of the experience of enlightenment disappear
And you let enlightenment,
Now empty and free of all remnants
Expand without limits.

3

An Introduction to the Knowledge of the Mind in the Tibetan Tradition

Some Features of Tantric Buddhism

Before starting the next series of meditations, I should say something about the history and particularities of Tibetan Buddhism, which includes Vajrayana ("Diamond Way"), Tantric Buddhism, esoteric Buddhism, or Mantrayana.

Buddhism practically disappeared from India for many centuries after the conquest by the Mongols (Islamized Mongol warriors), and today persists only in Sri Lanka and in nations neighboring India like Burma and Nepal—though before its near disappearance in India it had already migrated to Indonesia, China (from where it went to Korea and Japan), and Tibet.

Vajrayana or Tantric Buddhism, which would become the predominant form of Buddhism practiced in Tibet, entered the region in the 7th century and—due to the geographical circumstances of this so-called "Land of Snows"—was ultimately able to flourish there. Despite not being a country that built its military as much as some civilizations, the difficulty that Tibet's cold and mountains posed to invaders meant that the country was able to maintain its isolation with defenses in its border towns.

Tibet took a long time to allow Europeans to arrive. Alexandra David-Neel, a Belgian who published practically the first thing that was known about the culture, legends, and teachings of Tibet, managed to enter the country as a beggar and adopt a young lama. Then came Lama Govinda's classic on Tibetan mysticism. Lama Govinda had previously become a hermit in Sri Lanka and, after being invited to a religious meeting in Tibet, ended up staying in the country and converting to Vajrayana.

The important thing is that this mysterious country, due to its isolation and dedication to religious life, established itself as something that does not seem to have existed before or after in the world, and that only roughly could be called a theocracy. Unlike European theocracy in the Middle Ages or theocracy in Egypt, it was rather a "spiritual conservatory." I want to say that it was not so much a religious government as one in which there was great importance given to the training of lamas.

Just as there are countries that produce iron and countries that produce shoes or textiles, we can say that the most important thing that Tibet was producing was consciousness and experts in consciousness. And just as in the Middle Ages and until not so long ago in Europe, heads of family would send one of their children to be in the clergy (and another to the army and a third into trade), in Tibet it was a very coveted privilege to have one of your sons accepted into a monastery. It is no wonder, then, that in this country devoted mainly to growing consciousness, so many legends about miracles or extraordinary things were in circulation.

But just as when Buddhism migrated to China, a marriage between the Buddhist experience and traditional Taoist experience occurred, when Buddhism arrived to Tibet—a country that had developed a very high form of shamanism (the Bon religion)—it adopted certain ritualistic elements of the former spiritual tradition.

So just as the Taoist influence came to Tibet because of the proximity between Tibet and China during certain periods, some of its greatest masters came from the same mysterious region of Udiyana in which it is thought Bodhidharma was formed, and I understand that even Mesopotamian elements are found in the tantras.

You could say that Tibet became Buddhist in the eighth century when King Trisong Detsen felt inspired to bring in those who would boost this cultural transfer, an event which could be characterized as a planned revolution. For this, he invited the already famous Vimalamitra, but it is said that the great resistance coming from spiritual chieftains associated with the Bon culture made it advisable to invite the great sorcerer Padmasambhava, who is attributed with bringing to submission the divinities who have since served Buddhism.

Padmasambhava, founder of the oldest order of Buddhism in Tibet (The Nyingmapas or ancients) is, to this date, someone as revered in Tibet as the Buddha himself, because it is thought that only the teachings of Tantric Buddhism can have the power to rescue us from the greatest darkness that the world has been falling into in its history. But Buddhism lost influence and power in Tibet after its first centuries of life and recovered only after a new wave of influence coming from India through Naropa, who became a disciple of an Indian hermit named Tilopa. From Tilopa came a new lineage called the Kagyu, to which Milarepa (the best known of the saints of Tibet) belonged, and which also includes the lineage of the Karmapas. In addition, two further schools were created around this time: that of the Sakyapas and the Gelugpas (to which the Dalai Lamas, who were the political leaders of Tibet until a short time ago, have belonged).

I just mention these various schools or orders of Tibetan Buddhism to explain that the Chinese destroyed not just the monasteries and arts in Tibet, but also migrated its living religious culture to different parts of the world.

It seems like Padmasambhava's prophecy that says, "When horses run on rails and the iron bird flies through the sky, Buddhism will come to the land of the red man," has come true—because in our time of trains and planes, the land that once belonged to Indigenous people, which has become so powerful and so troubled, is showing a great deal of interest in Buddhism. It might also be thought that the forced exile of Tibetans could be benefiting the modern world with its presence, wisdom, and healing power. For as true as it is that, in our times, people are more absorbed in their survival than in the past and that increasing labor slavery is detrimental to people becoming interested in their healing transformation, it is also true that the future of humanity is in jeopardy, and that nothing can be as important to our future as the development of consciousness.

If we want to characterize Tibetan Buddhism through a comparison with the Theravada tradition or the Ch'an or Zen, one of the things that mostly gets our attention is its multifaceted and integrative character.

We can say that it works with a wide range of resources. And just as there are "broad spectrum" antibiotics, in the world of Tibetan meditation "there is a bit of everything," unlike the Vipassana and the Zazen traditions which have both grown monolithically with few variations. In contrast to the rather homogeneous or monochromatic flavor of these schools, the varied nature of Tibetan tradition could be said in a certain way to be multicolored. Although in the old Mahayana of India, the development of compassion—a characteristic of the ideal of Bodhisattva—had been highlighted, in Tantric Buddhism the devotional aspect is even more striking. It may even be said that in Tantric Buddhism you can see the yogic aspect of mental development (through stillness and introspection) and the devotional and ritual aspect, which becomes no less important than in Christianity and is expressed through great ceremonial wealth.

The wide palette of resources of Tibetan Buddhism includes such varied techniques as breathing exercises, visualization of deities, stimulating the flow of energy or prana through the chakras and the channels of the subtle body, and sexual yoga. But we can say that the pinnacle of the Tibetan teachings is reached in the explanations and practices aimed at understanding the nature of mind beyond mental phenomena.

The "technology of the sacred" in the Tibetan heritage covers a broad range of topics and these methods are part of the larger spectrum of the teachings. As alternative vehicles with progressive depth, one or another may be the most appropriate for a given individual at particular times during their development. Also, the notion of an enlightened person is different in Vajrayana in comparison to the ideals coming from Arhat and Bodhisattva.

I have already explained how the ideal of early Buddhism—the Arhat— is "one who has triumphed over his enemies" and we can interpret this as a transcendence of one's passions. The Bodhisattva of Mahayana, however (as we have seen), is one who has opened his heart to the recognition of his equality with everyone, which turns him into a person of great compassion, similar to the Christian saints. The ideal of Vajrayana, on the other hand, is called the Siddha, which refers to someone who has developed certain powers as a result of spiritual maturity.

There is a book containing summaries of the lives of the eighty-four legendary Mahasiddhas and in it you can see that, far from looking so perfect in their holiness, these great magicians of ancient Tibet were characterized by some seemingly negative traits. Of one, for example, it is said that he ate rotten fish. I think such stories contain symbolic allusions to various ways in which the spiritual path goes beyond conventional virtue. For when the mechanical quality of our own personality has already been overcome, certain aspects of it can be reintegrated for the benefit of all, similar to Jung's conception of a "reintegration of the shadow." Many seekers in the modern world have heard of Gurdjieff, the Russian teacher who differed from the most famous spiritual leaders because of his practicality and power. Tibetan monks also impress us as spiritual teachers who are not only knowledgeable guides for their disciples but can also function as feudal lords, addressing trade issues as much as the construction of a temple or the medical services of their village.

A spirit of innovation is also a feature of some of the mahasiddhas. A well-known lama, Khyentse Norbu—also known as Dzongsar Jamyang Khyentse Rinpoche—has produced a film called *The Cup* and there is also a film about him titled *Words of My Perfect Teacher*, which shows him interacting with people on a tram or leading his disciples to a stadium to practice detachment during the contemplation of a soccer match.

As in the famous Chinese images depicting stages of the inner journey through episodes about a grazing bull, we see the seeker return to the world—after he has completed his inner journey—as a normal person who can become invisible if he wants to.

First, he had to find the bull, which was initially not seen anywhere. Its tracks were barely seen from afar, until he was able to see it in the distance. Then the man mounts the bull that represents his own mind. We find an image in which the man and bull have both disappeared, but the realization of emptiness is not the end of the road, nor does the crystal clear fountain of flowing water, from which we can perceive iridescent reflections, represent the end of the road. This refers to the visionary world of Sambhogakaya and the last image shows a man who is approached with familiarity by children shopping in the market.

With this image of one who no longer notices that he has made the long journey, we see a person represented who has reached the end of the "period of fruition" in his transformation process. Even if this full maturity was understood in the Ch'an tradition, I have the impression that, especially in Tibetan Buddhism, teachers reach this level of spiritual development.

As Buddha says in one of his suttas, all methods are like the scaffolding of a house, which is no longer required once the house is built. We can, conversely, say that when spirituality is manifested in a very "spiritual" way, it is surely a sign that we are in the scaffolding stage.

Alternatively, when there is much talk about spiritual things, we are still in that phase of the inner journey during which one aspires to reach "the other side." There is, therefore, much thought about the vessel. For example, when people have been sailing for some time, they may talk of nothing else but masts, oars, knots, ropes, winds, and nautical arts. Those who have reached the other side, however, no longer speak about sailing or even the other bank, as they have understood that the other bank they aspired to reach is really the same it has always been—only now seen with more mature eyes. It is not only that their language has become less spiritual, but that the spiritual practices themselves seem to disappear, and the highest level of meditation ceases to be an intentional act or an exercise through which to manipulate your own mind. This is referred to as "non-meditation."

I would say that because of the maturity of so many monks and teachers, the condition of the mind in which spiritual thirst has been extinguished becomes instead the ability for joy, willingness to serve, and compassion, which has become part of Tibetan culture. You can say this especially of those who practice the Dzogchen or Ati Yoga, which is such a fast track that it is said that the result is obtained before starting the practice.

How can you say such a thing? Because the essence of this path is to understand that Buddhahood is already in oneself. Someone may say, "But what good is such a thing, if we already knew?"

But did we know?
And how do we get to know, then?

Once I asked the abbot of a monastery in Nepal for a certain instruction, and in response he said to me: "Look, I don't have as much experience as your own master, but you could go talk to my father." He was Chokyi Nyima Rinpoche, one of the children of the very famous master Tulku Urgyen, who no longer lives and whose autobiography called *Blazing Splendor* would be subsequently published. And he added: "He is not going to tell you anything you do not know, but when he explains it, one understands, because he has lived it so very deeply."

It is indeed true that when one speaks from deep experience, somehow such depth is apparent in the words one says. Put another way, the words somehow reflect the density of the experience from which one speak, and if one really knows something, it is different from the mere repetition of learned ideas or what is explained from a mere intellectual conviction.

Therefore, when the Sixth Patriarch Hui Neng said, "Your mind is the Buddha," it was enough for many to be enlightened. It was sufficient for him to explain that the Buddha is none other than the consciousness that is looking for the Buddha—many understood that and it changed their lives. Similarly, we can say that one of the characteristics of Tibetan Buddhism is the depth of understanding of their teachers, which allows for the transmission of correspondingly profound teachings. It is referred to as the power of the lineage.

And for this, a strong devotion is not only part of the way, but a particular devotion of the seekers toward the masters, who in turn have become depositories of the consciousness of the teachers who have preceded them.

Fritz Perls writes in his autobiography that when he visited a Zen master in Kyoto, he was disappointed that he bowed before an image of Avalokiteshvara, the Bodhisattva of compassion. He was seeking a godless Buddhism, and now discovered that Buddhists were too much like Christians. Of course his personality was such that he did not like to bow to anyone—the Tibetan way, which recognizes that we get blessings from those to whom we bow when they are actually transmitters of a lineage, would have been difficult for him.

There are also an abundance of allusions to sexuality in Tantric Buddhism, seen in many images that represent not only the Buddha but a Buddha or Bodhisattva in sexual union with his partner.

Why this omnipresence of sex in the representation of the enlightened mind? Because in enlightenment there is an element of joyful union of mind and world and the bliss of holiness has something to do with pleasure—the evocation of physical pleasure is not irrelevant to spiritual enjoyment.

And although sexual yoga is forbidden to those who have not practiced its preliminary elements, knowledge of sacred sex is in the spirit of Tantric Buddhism, unlike in most religions where the patriarchal spirit has led to the denial of the body.

It is also useful to know that in Tibetan Buddhism there are levels of education in which different explanations might seem contradictory in some respects, but must be understood in the same way as you can explain mathematical concepts from different points of view depending on the student's level of understanding. Thus, different levels of spiritual teaching may correspond to different ways of seeing things and different attitudes, ranging from austerity and discipline (as in Theravada) to greater self-giving.

Well, I've talked enough, but I just want to stress that within the wealth of elements of Tibetan Buddhism are practices as diverse as visualization, breathing exercises, reciting mantras, and physical practices. In the following sessions I will only be concentrating on meditation itself, and more specifically on the coupling of Shamata and Vipassana in view of the knowledge of the mind.

1

Bringing Together Shamata and Vipassana

We will begin this session by non-doing or Shamata, but with an
element of novelty: physical relaxation.
When the body is relaxed, the mind relaxes more easily.
It is not only easier for the mind to rest when the body is relaxed
but when the mind rests it no longer capitulates as much to
compulsive thinking or trying to get this or that.
First we seek to relax the mind from thought,
and then, with the mind now silent, let's move on to Vipassana,
turning our attention to the observation of the still mind.
But when the mind becomes still, what can one observe?
It would seem like a very reasonable instruction to "observe the
still mind" but in practice it may seem rather impossible,
since there is nothing to be found in a mind that has been stilled.
Observing one's own mind and finding nothing will soon become a
familiar experience.
But it usually happens that when we manage to quiet our mind
enough so "there is nothing,"
we lack the necessary subtlety to know *we are there.*
As it happens, the usual feeling of "ourselves" is very close to
feeling the body or, more broadly, to knowing that we are looking

97

at something. When we withdraw our attention from our body and our thinking we feel like we have disappeared.

But let us leave this subject of the *observation* of the mind at rest for a little later. First it is necessary that we release our thoughts, and we will begin with the physical relaxation that takes place when we release the muscle tone that is such a typical part of our ordinary experience that we don't even perceive it.

Speaking in scientific language, this chronic contracture of our muscular system (since the time of Wilhelm Reich) is called "body armor." Through the systematic awareness of this we can discover in it something like the reflection of our neuroses—our dysfunctional way of being in the world.

To begin, let's start by releasing the automatic gesture that follows us without us being aware of it: we will relax our facial muscles. I invite you to simply drop the mask that has stuck to your face ... So close is the relationship between the subtle mask we are used to wearing (an aspect of our self-image, of course) and our sense of identity, that when we relax our face muscles, it makes us feel as if we are disappearing.

Now I invite you to experiment with an even less familiar but very powerful element of relaxation: relaxation of the tongue.

Experiments have shown that relaxing your tongue helps to still the mind and it has also been shown through electromyography that when we think, we also speak, albeit unknowingly. The proof is that thought triggers electrical activity in the tongue and this can be interpreted as an indication that, as we think, we move our tongue subtly without the movements being evident.

Now we will relax our face and tongue at the same time, allowing the tongue to fall back slightly, as if we were going to swallow it. This will make us feel like toads, with a wider than usual neck, and perhaps with more awareness of the abdomen.

Just like the toad that has no neck, it would seem as if the tongue were rooted in the heart; as we drop the tongue we will surely feel that we become more aware of our heart.

It also happens that, by dropping the tongue, we feel the center of gravity of our whole body drop down and like toads we come closer to the ground.

Now I invite you to experiment with another aspect of relaxation that is clearly felt in our relationship with the world: the hands. What happens when we relax our hands?

To feel it, it is necessary to first truly relax them, which is difficult if we do not become aware of our chronic tension.

We cannot relax muscles we do not know are contracted and although the contraction in our hands is too habitual for us to perceive, we can induce relaxation of the hands by imagining that they are filled like sponges.

As you imagine, it might actually feel as if they swell a bit, since the visualization can bring the Prana or subtle energy to your hands. It is important to relax the hands because hands serve to grab things and meditation is a practice of detachment.

If we want to develop, then, an attitude of not clinging to anything, as befits the spirit of Buddhism (in which we aim not only to forgo attachments, but mental phenomena itself), it may be relevant to release the hands themselves.

Let us now try to do all three things at once: relaxing the face, relaxing the tongue, and dropping the hands.

Now I suggest doing the same thing with your feet.

We don't even know how much tension we carry in our feet, which have almost become as hooves from always having them inside shoes. They are the most difficult to relax because they have become very insensitive.

But it is said that the Buddhas have "lotus feet."
Why?

Because through the process of releasing the body, as we are able to let go from top to bottom—opening the body gradually, ending in our feet—we may recover the softness we associate with the foot of a child.

If we open our feet to the descending energy that seems to enter our body through the crown of the head, such that we release the voluntary control over our body, we can come to feel like a channel between heaven and earth—an open channel that makes us feel lighter.

One gets to fully enjoy this stillness of becoming a channel, now that it is no longer an effort but more like coming home.
We do not have to know anything, not even when we can leave the world behind. As we let go of the stress of daily life, it is natural that we find the stillness inherently pleasurable.

But now we will add to this physical relaxation, the relaxation of the usual intention of getting something.
You need to let go of the idea of any accomplishment, and stop moving toward some future goal.
Perhaps before sitting down to meditate, we intended to get closer to enlightenment, but now that we meditate, we must understand that meditation involves not finding anything other than what the river of life brings us moment to moment. Letting the river of life pass through us without seizing anything, or even believing that we are something ...
we relax our breathing, too, surrendering to its spontaneous rhythm. We observe our breath just enough to know whether it is quiet or not, and if we find that there is effort or impatience in the way we breathe, we set that aside, allowing our breathing to happen on its own, any way it wants.

Surely we have already established enough stillness to make us feel, at times, that our mind has stopped. And although we may not

have more than moments of silence and inner stillness, I invite you
to observe these moments, inquiring how an empty mind feels.
Is an empty consciousness possible?
Let us now prepare to slowly open our eyes, without losing our
focus on the silence.
Take advantage of the fact that with open eyes one is a little more
awake, and this allows us to pay greater attention to the empty mind.
I invite you to look more towards the periphery of the visual field
than toward the center.
And we begin looking up very slowly, keeping the gaze panoramic,
feeling the space in all directions.
Just as we usually rest our gaze on a single point, we can also rest
while directing our gaze everywhere at once.

And if we let our gaze dissolve in space, it will also allow our mind
to dissolve or evaporate.
We identify our mind with space.
Now we go to meet the other's gaze, always with a loose body, loose
hands, loose face, without seeking anything.
And even if only briefly, we let the contagious aspect of meditation
operate through this meeting of the eyes.
When one meditates well, it is possible that one's own state
becomes spontaneously an inspiration to the other. When
one does not, it is then possible for one to be inspired by someone
who has gone further in dropping the body to the ground,
dissolving the mind in space.

2

The Mirror, the Crystal, and Space

People say they meditate "to quiet their mind" or that they meditate "to become more aware," but we do not only meditate to get respite from the whirlwind of life or to know what happens in our mind and body. In the best of cases, we want to answer that famous question that we in the West associate with the Oracle of Apollo at Delphi: "Who are you?"

"Know thyself," commanded the Oracle to Socrates, and Socrates took it upon himself to stimulate interest in such knowledge among his contemporaries. But I don't think that the knowledge of self that the Oracle prescribed referred to an understanding of *how* we are, to knowledge of our personality and relationships, or even the persistence of our past in our present.

What was surely meant by such a legendary mandate was something like, "Know who you are *behind* your personality," or: "Who are you beyond the things you do and the roles you play?"

Not everyone feels compelled to answer this question of "Who are you?," which amounts to a search for truth, or a search for something that is true on its own, and not by participation in something else.

The academics do not acknowledge the Greeks or their oracle for such a profound question and believe that, in urging people to know themselves, they intended only a warning to keep in mind their human and mortal condition without falling into the exaltation of hubris.

I think the issue of self-knowledge was so important to the Greeks because it was no different for them than the pursuit of the "original face" in the Zen tradition—only that in Buddhism this search is undertaken through a paradoxical renunciation of imagination and a concentration on non-doing.

This is even more explicit in Tibetan Buddhism, in which an experiential encounter with the mystery is sought through a convergence of non-doing and seeing: a cognition of the mind itself beyond mental phenomena.

This is what is called "wisdom"— a term corresponding to that of *gnosis* in the Western world, or knowledge of "the Truth," the "Divine," or the "Spiritual." But we might perhaps just say that a metaphysical thirst drives some of us to seek "the invisible world"— in reference to a domain of the mind not perceptible to the intellect. But how can we access such knowledge of the mysterious depths of the mind and reality?

Already the disciples of the Buddha knew —and also the yogis of ancient India knew it—that this requires a quiet mind but also (and this was what the Buddha especially emphasized) the development of special focusing capacity.

Yet even a mind trained in focusing (through Vipassana) and in stillness (through Shamata) needs something else: the "teachings" for which Tibetan Buddhism is so remarkable—explanations given about what is not properly explicable.

What is sought in meditation is indescribable, and after recognizing it we may feel that it makes little sense to continue being interested in words.

But don't we know how many words Zen Buddhism has produced about the ineffable? They are difficult to understand, it is true, and also true that speech that proceeds from the ineffable may only be understood by those already familiar with its experience—to which words may only be pointers.

All attempts at explanation, then, are only intended to serve as a bridge for those who do not yet know firsthand what they are looking for, much as it happens in art, which only opens its meaning to those who have already had the experience that it wants to communicate.

For, true as it is that art tells us something, we can only grasp something that is a step beyond what we have already grasped, and not much else. We need to grow, to understand art, and then art grows in us.

Do you understand what I mean?

Just as art displays and at the same time conceals, so that what we imperfectly understand gradually becomes a path to further understanding for us, so it is with Buddhist scriptures and the teachings that they transmit.

And not only with Buddhist scriptures, but all the writings that seek to communicate the mystical domain of human experience.

Even of the Gospels, which seem so simple, you can say the same. What is said about "the truth" through parables, for instance, is more difficult to understand than what people think, and this goes unnoticed because we are so familiar with them.

When it is said, for instance, "the truth shall set you free," we might believe that this refers to ordinary truth, much as when we affirm that sincerity or authenticity helps us in getting to know ourselves better or heal our relationships.

Examination of the apocryphal Gospels, however, has made it clear that the *truth* of which the Gospel speaks is the same as that in Buddhism, which speaks to us about a "deep truth" beyond the apparent, common sense or scientific truth of things, and which refers to the congruence of statements and facts—even beyond time and space.

It is a truth that Buddha also called "the un-originated," assuring us that in the knowledge of this truth we may find peace and happiness.

We may say that it is glimpses of this profound truth that have given birth to almost all philosophy—for even though we have known both idealistic and materialistic philosophies, what originally motivated those who were called "philosophers" (i.e.,"lovers of wisdom") was the intuition of the mystery of a transcendent realm.

For it has been claimed that the knowledge of this mystery not only makes seekers wise but, nourishing their mind more deeply than any worldly object of desire, it frees them from their afflictions.

Not only does Buddhism affirm the existence of this "deeper truth" that is at the bottom of all things, but it tells us that it may be found deep within ourselves, so that whoever seeks into the depth of his own mind may come to this absolute level of reality.

We may call it God but we know that, in the context of Christian culture, God is presented as very distant and that it is even taboo to think that one may be divine.

Alan Watts, the great intellectual of the Sixties who was, for the culture of California, a sort of cultural hero who brought into the West an interest in the Tao and in Zen Buddhism, said that if a Westerner says "I am God" he will be sent to an asylum but that in India—where the identification of the soul (or Atman) with the Divine (Brahman) is so ingrained—if someone says he has discovered that he is God, he is congratulated for finally having realized it.

Yet in Buddhism, we speak of Buddhahood rather than God. And it is also said that we are all Buddhas and that the only difference between Buddhas and other beings is that Buddhas *know* that they are Buddhas, while the rest have not realized it as a result of a potentially reversible blindness.

Such is the quest for wisdom, then: to find that profound truth underlying all things, which is the only thing we may truly call "reality."

We might also call it Being, but Buddhism is so reluctant to intellectualizations that it prefers to say that it is "neither being nor non-being" and even denies that it is both, or none.

It wants to emphasize through these statements (attributed to Nagarjuna) that transcendent reality has nothing to do with our concepts and that, from the moment we affirm the relationship of emptiness with something we are wrong—for not even emptiness is "empty."

In other words, that "nature of mind" which is sought through the practice of meditation is something that is not on any map and is not something we might point to, saying that it is *this* or *that*.

Though it might seem that nothing can be said about the ineffable, there are teachings in the Tibetan Buddhist tradition that make it possible for seekers to find sooner that which cannot be described— and aside from the preliminary mind-training of Shamata and mindfulness, the most useful teachings are presented in the form of three images, which we may also conceive to be metaphors.

One of them invites us to contemplate the mind as a mirror.

It seems as if the idea that the mind is like a mirror that reflects things in the outer world is something well-known and sufficiently understood. But to be useful, the mirror needs to be explained in such a way that it can inspire in us a different point of view concerning our experiences than the usual one.

For ordinarily, while seeing what we see or while feeling what we feel, we implicitly believe that the flow of our experiences is our "self," or identity.

Yet when we regard our experiences as something comparable to what is reflected in a mirror, and then regard our mind as the mirror itself, we may then proceed to understand that our "mirror-like mind"—beyond its contents—is perfectly neutral, and then the notion of the mirror's neutrality may help us grasp the nature of our consciousness itself.

Let us say that I am in a state of depression, boredom, or apathy, and this is stopping me from meditating. I have been implicitly identifying with such a state, but if I adopt the point of view that my boredom or depression are one thing, while my consciousness is another—comparable to a mirror that contains what it reflects without being affected by it—I may feel relieved.

For once I adopt this point of view, according to which experiences such as happiness, sadness, anger, ambition, indifference, or depression are just objects or contents in the field of a consciousness (which, like a mirror, is by nature immutable), this *will allow me a shift in identity* through which I will not only have distanced myself from my painful perceptions or emotions, but come to identify with consciousness itself.

The invitation to understand that things that are reflected in a mirror are not only other than the mirror, but that the mirror is not even *interested* in them (because it stays indifferent to both beauty and ugliness) may inspire us to become as immutable or neutral as the mirror itself, and even discover in the process that *something as neutral and empty as a mirror is already in us*, as the very subject of our consciousness.

If we liken the world of human experience to what is reflected in a mirror and can at least glimpse that the mirror—beyond the things it reflects—*is free* of the things it reflects, we may also conceive that the drama of life is like a film that passes through the glass lens of a film projector.

We may be moved by the film, but we must recognize that it does not exist separately from the light that animates its images.

Instead of identifying with the flow of life, then, we may imagine that our mind is like a crystal through which life passes.

And once we identify with the empty field through which our mental events flow, we also dis-identify with the display of thinking, feeling, and willing.

What are we, then? The life-stream?

Or the space through which it flows?

While in therapeutic culture (and specifically for Fritz Perls, the father of Gestalt Therapy), the "Self" is "the here and now" or the flow of our present experience, Buddhism invites us to replace our usual identification with our experience with that of an empty field through which there flows the story we call "I."

The characters in our movie can feel all kinds of emotions and the movie has its sad, happy, or terrifying moments, but if we are able to look at ourselves as the clear field through which the film flows, we can feel a peaceful detachment.

Buddhism is a religion of non-attachment, as are yoga and Vedanta, containing the same wisdom which allows people who have lived long enough to no longer be conditioned by their passions. "Like a child who leaves behind his old toys when he no longer needs them," goes an often repeated analogy—life itself may mature us, so that we learn to look at things from a greater distance and with more perspective.

But the essence of non-attachment is dis-identification, so that our attempts to let go of our passions or dysfunctional habits are not likely to succeed unless we come to understand them to be extraneous to our true identity.

Those who know the work of Gurdjieff will be familiar with the prescription not to identify with their own fleeting experience but it is also difficult to go very far with the mere concept of dis-identification or with the prescription: "do not identify"—whereas this comes by itself once we identify with the mirror of our own consciousness.

If I don't want to be in the grip of my anger, for example, I will surely realize how difficult it is not to do so once my anger "takes over." But if I manage to identify with my empty and neutral consciousness, which is my fundamental nature, beyond any specific mental phenomena, I can see that even though there is anger *in* me, I *am not* the anger.

If the image of a mirror functions as a living metaphor when we use it to discriminate between consciousness and its contents, so it is with space.

It is said already in early Buddhism that what most resembles Nirvana is space. This means that there is a "mental space," a space of consciousness that we ordinarily fail to perceive and in which all our experiences are contained. Yet instead of living ourselves as space, we seem to forget about it, much as we forget that in the concrete world we live in space and sometimes we are barely aware of the space beyond a sort of cocoon surrounding our skin—as if we were too absorbed in ourselves to perceive the infinite universe that we inhabit.

Yet space sometimes seems to make itself present to us in certain environments, and then we feel that something in our mind shifts. If we enter a cathedral, for example, where the architecture is specially designed to make us feel small in a large space, we not only perceive space over our heads, but may also perceive our heads more—just as it is the case when certain hats are worn, such as those of the Dervishes or medieval magicians, that have the effect of making us feel as if our heads were to extend upward.

A starry night can also subtly affect the way in which we perceive space. Sometimes, of course, nothing touches us, and we are just indifferent to all that goes on beyond our skin, but there are times when we are open, and on a night when many stars are visible, we may have a sense of the vastness of space—a mysterious depth of the universe.

One could easily say that this is an "aesthetic" experience, but perhaps it is too superficial to call it that, because anybody who contemplates the experience of a starry sky and its immensity will recognize that it also involves something like feeling insignificant by contrast.

And anybody who knows what it is like to feel a bit like an ant will recognize that one's problems are no longer so important—as if space had an effect of neutralizing stress.

So that, by just remembering that the universe is immense, we may be inspired to see things differently and we could therefore say it is therapeutic to look at things from the perspective of the stars.

It is similar to what some astronauts have described when reporting on their experience of seeing the Earth from afar. For some, it has been enough to change their life. One may have read about such reports and regarded them as merely "subjective," not understanding that the sheer vastness of space can induce non-attachment, and non-attachment is the gateway of Enlightenment.

Just conceiving of a large space is already a form of meditation, then, and there are visualization practices in the Hindu tradition where one imagines a lotus, first the usual size, then larger and larger, up to the size of the room, then the whole house, then the village, the horizon, and finally of cosmic proportions.

But can we visualize a rose with the dimensions of the distance from here to the sun?

The light that seems to come to us from the sun in an instant actually takes no less than eight minutes to reach us at its speed of one hundred and eighty six thousand miles per second.

And can we imagine a rose the size of the planetary system?

I once asked an astronomer what size the atoms in our body would be if we were the size of the planetary system and he calculated more or less the size of tennis balls.

If one imagines oneself at the scale of the planetary system, one will become a dance of apples or tennis balls—each one consisting mainly of empty space and almost invisible particles of questionable materiality.

Also, with such a change of scale it is difficult to maintain a physical image, because when an atom is the size of a tennis ball, the electron is not yet visible. If one wants to be more realistic (and this is only looking at things at a different scale), we will perceive ourselves as a dance of electrons not only invisible, but rather immaterial.

My teacher, Tarthang Tulku Rinpoche, has proposed an exercise to imagine the size of the planetary system, which goes beyond being an evocation of the immense, for it also leads us to glimpse that we *are* space—much like how Einstein proposed that matter and energy are crystallizations of the geometry of space. If we succeed in visualizing it (that is, imagining it deeply), we may come to feel that there is nothing to worry about. What a relief!

It is like the "peace of the dead," so feared until we discover it—perhaps by imagining ourselves without a body, emotions, or thoughts.

Are we perhaps not mistaken in fussing so much about dying when we come from space and to space we ultimately return?

But then, there is a whole way of meditating that is like reframing our experience to include its space-basis.

We may begin by feeling the space that is here, within the walls of this room, and then try to conceive of the cosmic space, that has no limits.

Summing up: can we not go beyond an attention to our immediate experience by including an awareness of space? But perhaps I have said enough for now as a prologue to a second guided meditation, which I will explain one step at a time.

3

Vipassana from the Perspective of Space

Pair up with someone, and as in past meditation sessions take advantage of the opportunity to get to know different people through situations of silent contact in meditation.

I do not know if all of you who are here have heard an explanation of the gesture we make before and after the meditation, when we bow with our palms joined in front of our chest. You may know it as *Pranam,* as it is called in India, or as *Gasho* in Japan and zen environments. It has a different meaning before meditation than it does at the close of a session.

Before meditation, it is a gesture of surrender, as in the refuge; a gesture of both surrender and reverence, as in getting out of the way when you approach something bigger. If I want to approach something bigger, it is appropriate that I get rid of any sense of personal importance, which would be out of place, and in this spirit I bow.

At the end of meditation, however, when we once more make the same gesture, it means that if we have reached something of value through meditation, it behooves us to share with others the corresponding merit. This brief ritual gesture is actually now called "dedication of merit," and we may regard it as a way of continuing to be consistent with the spirit of meditation—for wanting to hoard the meditation's merit would be contrary to the spirit of the practice, which is that of non-attachment.

Without this act of giving away the merit that we have achieved through our time of sitting, effort, and dedication, our ego might want to cling to it as a sort of spiritual curriculum on a race to enlightenment comparable to someone who wants to be accredited, like a pilot who comes closer to getting his license by accumulating flight hours. Thus, by dedicating the merit that we have acquired, we keep the results of meditation pure and free from selfish or narcissistic contamination.

There are many ways of dedicating merit, but let's leave that for now to the discretion of each of you. Sometimes there is a sick person in your life, or someone who you want to help, but this gift can also be offered to all beings, or radiated to all awakened beings or Buddhas, who are said to reside in all directions of space—so that they can manage our "grain of sand" as they see fit.

But now let us move on to the meditation itself, and let us start with non-doing, which is to say, with no intention of achieving anything.

Surely we are aware of being here, in this place and time, and we allow ourselves the restfulness of not having to fill our field of experience with anything. We are simply here, and we let ourselves be as we are.

When one does nothing, breathing usually makes itself more present than in ordinary life.

And being conscious of our breath does not take away from our sense of being present, but rather helps us feel every moment. Also, the air we breathe in and out invites us to not remain on the surface of our body.

And similarly, it also seems that the awareness of the breath invites
us toward the center of our being, or toward the depth of our
consciousness.

Surely we are feeling this way or that
—either good, bad, or indifferent—
but we know that meditation is not about trying to be a certain way,
but to accept being as we are.

All possible states of mind are compatible with meditation,
because meditation has nothing to do with what you feel or see,
but with your attitude.
And it is not what you see that matters most, but from where
you're looking.

An unattached, neutral point of view is recommended,
like that of a mirror in regard to what is reflected on its surface.
I invite you, then, to take seriously the idea
that we are not what is before us,
but rather, that everything we perceive exists in consciousness.

Beyond what we feel, beyond the thoughts that go through the
space of our consciousness, let us adopt the point of view that we
are the field that contains all of our experiences—
and see if we can be inspired by this idea of the mirror to become
more immutable,
or to discover that there is always something unalterable in us,
for even if a mirror is somehow invisible when stripped away of
what it is reflecting
—a pure emptiness—
we may also discover in this emptiness the most stable thing there is.

If in dis-identifying from the objects of consciousness
we identify with consciousness itself,
it is not difficult to come to feel invulnerable.

Whatever happens in the world of reflections,
no matter what happens inside our mind,
we are like the space that allows everything to be.

And space is pure permeability.
Space can teach us a transparent and open way to be in the world.
Things are no longer ugly or beautiful, or good and bad,
and once we accept everything,
nothing feels threatening.
Nothing can threaten our existence when we become like space.
But can we, when we become space, still talk about our own
existence?

I invite you to continue to observe the present, becoming aware of
what appears from moment to moment, yet from the perspective
that "we" are something like the space that contains not only our
emotions and impulses,
but even our body. Because our body also exists within our consciousness, which is nothing and supports everything.

The effort to silence thinking also disappears
when one is the space that contains our thoughts.
Even if thoughts pass through us,
they do not distract us from our identification with the field of
consciousness.

Leave behind, then, the idea that we are inside a body,
perhaps in our brain,
or in our heart, or wherever,
and think, rather, that we are a space that has no limits
and contains everything.

As we continue our Vipassana practice,
noticing our present experience from the perspective of space,
we experience whatever happens in the moment

as something that exists within a space that is the
field of consciousness.
And now we can allow ourselves no longer to be concerned so much
with the *what*, or even the *how*, but with the *where*:
the space-consciousness we are.

And now take the step from meditating with closed eyes to meditating with open eyes, and try to do so with care so that this
transition does not distract us from what we are doing—which is
to live the moment from the perspective of space.

And surely we will discover that adopting the perspective of space
is easier with eyes open, since physical space reminds us of the
space of consciousness with which we are identifying.
Feel the space within this room.
And now imagine the space surrounding this room.
And then imagine the horizon.
And also imagine a dome that has the horizon for its base.
And also imagine the space around that dome.

Now imagine an inverted dome inside the Earth, symmetrical
to the dome that we are visualizing above the horizon, so that
a sphere is formed between the two of them: a space that in its
bottom half is filled by rock and earth instead of air, but which is
incorporeal, as is the nature of space.

By now perhaps our body is somewhat tired, our attention may
have become fatigued, our legs may be in pain—but let us take
advantage of these annoyances to pay particular attention to
whatever is uncomfortable, unsatisfactory, or painful at this time,
looking at it from the perspective of space.
Can we see that one thing is what hurts and another, at the same
time, is the neutrality of pure consciousness?

The act of perceiving is an act of noticing and nothing else, perfectly clear and dispassionate, so that if we become space-like, we may feel that something hurts without our usual compulsion to avoid it. When we make space to become permeable to everything, we may also learn to become space-like.

So let us continue holding the view that we are a nothing pierced by everything.

The stream of life goes through us, but we are a pure openness. And now let us continue to hold the same attitude with our eyes open. Yet slowly approaching the encounter with our partner through the gaze, as we continue attending to the here and now, identifying with an infinite field that is nothing of what happens in it, but a pure container.
Look from behind your eyes, with a deeper look than that of your habitual identity ...
As if you were an extraterrestrial intelligence.
One not from here.
A view from nowhere, that because of its pure neutrality
may also feel as if it were the look of the dead.
And let us try to be more interested in *who* is looking than in what appears before our eyes,
focused more on the *subject* of consciousness than on
what is being perceived.

4

From the Awareness of Mental Phenomena to the Awareness of Awareness

Before I say anything, and before we start to meditate, let us observe how it is to not have even begun to meditate.

And now let us begin to meditate, according to the instruction of "not doing anything."

In other words, we leave ourselves in peace.

Or, in other words, we allow ourselves to be as we are

without any attempt to manipulate our ongoing experience.

It is hard to go on for long before becoming aware of our breathing, which is part of non-doing.
Just as we breathe during our sleep,
we also breathe while letting ourselves "be as we are."

But in becoming aware of your breath, let it happen by itself, without falling into the temptation of controlling it.

We know that sometimes non-doing becomes an effort,
like swimming against the stream
of our automatic activity,
but there are times when we find another way of non-doing,
which is like the simple pleasure of resting.
Something like sinking inward
and letting the mind go wherever it wants to be.
It is as if our mind wants to go home,
which is back to itself,
after having been imprisoned by the world and its demands.
And when we allow ourselves to rest from our projects,
we leave it in freedom to return to its center,
and to its natural state of stillness.
Once stillness is achieved
and we can already perceive the taste of rest,
become aware of your body.
There are many ways to become aware of the body,
and one of them is feeling the whole body.
Surely feeling the whole body, from head to toe,
is something we all felt as children, but have lost.
Just as our psyche has lost its unity, we have also lost the
experience of an integrated body,
and when we bring our attention to our whole body
we notice that there are parts that we feel more, and others less.
We naturally feel drawn to give more attention to the parts
we feel less, as if trying to be more present in them, or to bring
them to more aliveness.
This practice of simply being with the sense of the whole body
could be enough for a meditation session,
and whole meditation retreats are dedicated by Theravadins to
nothing beyond sensing.
But just as we have taken not-doing as a starting point, and sought
not to interrupt our restfulness in attending to our breath and body,

let us now retain awareness of our body as a backdrop to the following guided meditation, even as we begin to notice our emotional state.

Positive emotions—the pleasure of the moment—and also negative emotions—the displeasure or dissatisfaction of the moment.
We probably notice a certain specific atmosphere in us
which is like a well-known or chronic state.
Perhaps a discomfort that is reflected in our body as a shrinking,
or as a tension, or perhaps as nausea or boredom ...
Let us try to identify this problematic emotional atmosphere.
And now let us simply observe when we are thinking
and also when we are not.
Let us try to see how our thoughts begin
and how they end.
Always doing nothing but noticing
our body, our emotional state,
and what happens in our thinking,
and looking at what happens between one thought and the next.
What is there?
And how is that?
Could that be consciousness itself?

We have surely noticed the problem of observing
consciousness itself.
If we manage to observe the space between one thought
and another,
it seems that there is nothing there,
and yet we are not in a coma.
And although you don't see anything,
it is as if you were in a dark room
where, in spite of seeing nothing,
you know very well that you are there.

I invite you to observe this "knowing that you are there," trying to
savor it.
What is that? Is our feeling of our presence only an awareness of
our breath?
Or a tactile awareness?
Body awareness?
Or do we perceive our pure mind in stillness?

The Mahayana experience indicates that our perceptions, thoughts,
emotions, desires, and other mental events exist in the field of
our consciousness, which is like a space beyond body and thought,
beyond mental phenomena.

And we may know theoretically that that this field of consciousness
itself, is nothing other than the "Buddha nature" we seek.
We have been told by those, whose path has come to fruition,
that our spiritual thirst longs for something we already are,
and is the ground of our perceptions and actions.
Yet just as we cannot see our own eyes,
the subject of consciousness seems unable to perceive itself.

But we do expect a meeting of consciousness with itself,
though we are already mistaken in approaching it as "our" mind,
since we do not own that mind that we seek,
but rather belong to it.

In any case, just as in the Hindu tradition the inquiry concerning
the self is recommended, in the Tibetan tradition it is also recommended that we pose the question: *where is the mind?*

Let's now make the transition into meditation with open eyes
but without distraction from the task of inquiring *who is searching*.
Or, alternatively, we seek *who is meditating*.

Who aspires to awaken?

Allow for a very slow transition between opening your eyes and
finding your partner's gaze.
But do not get distracted from the pursuit of the subject of your
own consciousness.

It is not by looking that you may achieve it, because when we "look"
we are already making a distinction between subject and object.

It is as if to find ourselves we have to resort to a sense other
than sight.

Perhaps we need to do something like sinking into ourselves, or
rather, allowing ourself to be swallowed by a greater self
and then becoming it.

You "remember yourself," it is said in the Sufi world,
in which it is also claimed that "to know oneself is to know God."

And now I invite you to see if it is possible to feel yourself and
at the same time feel that the person sitting in front of you is
seeing you.
In other words, relate to the other as not just a body,
but as a consciousness, an existence.

5

Entering Meditation with Compassion Through an Appeal to Avalokiteshvara

Music, apart from the recitation of the sutras, is not used much in the Buddhist tradition, but in Tibetan Buddhism, rituals often contain musical interludes that create a context favorable for meditation. It is just that such musical episodes are quite different from what we call "music" in the Western world.

I will now play for you a commercially available recording that is part of a collection of songs by Yungchen Lhamo, a version of the well known Om Mani Padme Hum mantra.

You surely know that in Tibetan Buddhism it is thought that the pursuit of wisdom through meditation must be accompanied by the cultivation of compassion, which is expressed in the life of personal relationships.

You might say that compassion is an alternative way to the undoing of ego-centeredness. In Buddhism it is thought that—since the ego does not exist—it is not that the ego has to be fought, so much as we come to realize that it is illusory.

And not only in Buddhism: I had a well-known teacher, Swami Muktananda, who once asked me to publish a little book of his called *Getting Rid of What You Haven't Got*—which might be reworded as "free yourself from what you don't have" or "free yourself of this idea that you have of a personal ego." So Buddhism is not so unique in inviting us to dispel the illusion of ego.

But what the Buddhist tradition recommends is that, on the one hand, we cultivate the wisdom of non-ego (or the wisdom of a cosmic identity that is not the identity of this little character who gives us so much trouble) and, on the other hand, we cultivate compassion.

These two aspects of the path in Buddhism are represented through the two ritual objects in the hands of Vajrasattva—the Buddha representing *Dharmadhatu,* or the space of all phenomena. And we may say that wisdom not only leads to compassion, but that compassion also helps us in coming to wisdom.

The Eightfold Path already prescribes that meditation goes hand in hand with virtue and understanding, and in this it coincides with Christianity, which considers mystical experience as the blossoming of a love-oriented life.

Yet, conversely, wisdom leads to compassion, since compassion is already in our nature, though blocked by egocentrism.

If we came to understand that we don't exist, wouldn't this imply the disappearance of our excessive preoccupation with ourselves and our privileges?

If compassion leads to wisdom and wisdom to compassion, then, it behooves us to deal with both, and I usually explain the importance of compassion on the spiritual path with the famous Cuban song that says:

> *To get to heaven you need*
> *one long staircase and a short one.*[2]

Contemplation is the short ladder, because it is as if the truth were always before us, only we are blindfolded, and so it is enough to take that blindfold away by putting our life in order. The purification process of straightening our psyche and our relationships—that is the

---

2 Para llegar al cielo se necesita
una escalera larga y una cortita.

long staircase, the "purification of sins" of Christianity, not unlike what in Buddhism is known as the liberation from the Kleshas.

Let us say, in short, that it is easier to come to heaven if one is interested in becoming a good person.

Enlightenment will not be so easy, however, if what moves us is not the desire to serve but the desire to achieve a position of superiority over those who have not been enlightened.

So if you need to become a more loving person to reach spiritual success, is it not also true that even in a specific meditation session we will do better if we go into it with a loving attitude?

In other words, it matters for meditation that in addition to the actual instructions we keep attitude in mind as an aspect that works as an inspiring factor.

Let us now apply a corollary to this view that not only do our yogic abilities help to quiet the mind and concentrate our attention, but also that we need to be good people.

This corollary is that it is not irrelevant to meditation that we undertake it with a loving attitude.

But are we able to be more compassionate than we are right now? And how may we develop compassion?

I do not know, among the resources of contemporary psychology, a better way to become a more loving person than to give up the hatred, resentment, and feelings of revenge we hold in response to the sufferings of our childhood in regards to our parents, since in all our adult relationships the patterns established during our relationship with them are repeated.

As Freud observed, we seek in all our loving relationships the love of our original relationship with our mother, and our relationship with authority is reflected in all our working relationships, which were originally represented by our father.

But we have already done a good job with the cleaning up, which began with the awareness about how our personality was formed during our childhood.

By reopening old wounds, we have allowed ourselves to relive our early childhood rage, and then proceed to decriminalize it, and also to understand and forgive our parents. And this has certainly improved our relationship with our parents and others in our environment, but it is also true that we need to continue giving attention to the development of compassion.

But how? I think the most important thing in becoming more compassionate is to be deeply interested.

We must come to understand that being compassionate is a very good thing for ourselves, and not just because it is a noble ideal or because religions preach love, or because Buddhism recommends it or Islam says that God himself is merciful.

For it is not an efficient enough motivation to want to be compassionate because everyone else says so, nor because it is mandated by the authorities.

I think that it may be best to understand it from the perspective of our own selfishness. In addition, one must have lived enough to realize the bad results of *not* having compassion.

If you are full of hate, you will know the unhappiness of it. And one day you will realize that the happiness you seek is a state of love and once you have understood that happiness comes from the expression of one's loving potential, it is possible that you will become very interested in developing the capacity to love, which entails being interested in others and in helping.

Compassion is just one of the forms of love, but apparently, the most difficult.

It goes beyond a simple, "I hope you have a good time," and involves both the desire that another does not suffer intensely and the desire to help lessen someone's suffering, which implies some measure of sacrifice.

Compassion requires some measure of identification and empathy; a sense that because the other is an equal he matters. And I don't know how it is for you, but I would like to "open my heart more," as is sometimes said, to come to have a bigger heart. And I think it would be good for me to be able to forgive more (even if when we forgive another on account of some specific issue, we should also forgive ourselves).

But aside from the matter of motivation, Tibetan Buddhism offers a *magical* way: that of appealing to someone who already has compassion, and is not from this world.

We might think of compassion as a universal energy that we may connect with, similar to music, and remember the nature of a self-less form of love we call "compassion" or "mercy."

This seems to us the most satisfying feeling for it is as if we then became more fully human.

Yet aside from such moments, it is as if we have forgotten what compassion is like despite having a word for it. And how could we put into practice something that we have forgotten about?

We need compassion to be present so that we remember it and we can give ourselves to it, wishing that our will is in resonance with the suffering of others.

That presence of compassion or mercy (personified in the Christian tradition in the figure of Mary, mother of God), is embodied in Mahayana Buddhism in the Bodhisattva Avalokiteshvara (personified by the Chinese in female form as Kuan Yin).

Avalokiteshvara is represented as a figure with a thousand arms, in reference to the myth wherein his arms were granted the ability to multiply in order to meet the needs of all beings. And in each hand he had an eye, signifying a compassionate attention to such needs.

This figure that personifies compassion can help us consider that compassion is not something we need to create or produce, but is already in the world, even when we are not connected with it.

In other words, the image of a deity invites us to imagine a deposit of energy potentially accessible to us.

But how? And here comes the magical aspect of Buddhism: through mantras, which are a way to contact entities that may be likened to email addresses. Mantras are essentially incantations, which we mostly associate with medieval romances and legendary figures such as Merlin, and have come to be regarded today as little more than mumbo jumbo.

Of such magic formulas or incantations, which usually consist of the names of certain entities such as the angels of the Judeo-Christian tradition or the "names of God," we can say that the main one in the Hindu-Buddhist tradition is **Om**, which has the evocative power of wholeness or the universal sound of a gong, and which invites us to evoke a sacred depth.

But Om is often used as part of other longer mantras, in a way comparable to that of building sentences with words.

The mantra of compassion is this type of mantra and constitutes a call to Avalokiteshvara: Om Mani Padme Hum.

It is often simply called the Mani, and if you have been to Nepal you will have seen it engraved on the large rocks near the pilgrimage path leading to the famous and archaic Swayambhu Stupa.

The word Mani means jewel, but in a way mantras are untranslatable even though their elements are associated with certain meanings. They work in a way similar to poetry, which needs words and not just ideas.

I think that it may help you understand this statement about poetry being made of words and not just ideas if I tell you of a conversation that I had long ago with a Chilean poet, in which I argued that the most important thing in a poem is the content, and too much concern about words was a questionable refinement.

Wanting to defend that poetry is created with words, he gave me this verse as an example:

Heartbroken by his sad fate,
he drank the tears and the wine.

Then he repeated the same content with the following alternative vocabulary:

Heartbroken by his sad fate,
he drank the tears and the chicha.

It is hard to convey the matter in an English translation, but perhaps it will be appreciated that the change from "wine" to "chicha" (cider) does away with the nobility of the earlier statement. Something of a similar nature happens with mantras, which we may call "phonetic symbolism."

Literary critics usually have a keen ear for it, and I remember reading a comment by Damaso Alonso about a Góngora verse that says:

"Infame turba de nocturnas aves."

His commentary explained that the verse, like a bird with white wings, starts with an "A" (in *infame*) and ends with "A" (in *aves*), but carries in its middle part the "U" sound (*Infame turba de nocturnas aves*). The sound A-U-U-A, then suggested a night bird whose body is dark but whose wings are white.

Through this phenomenon of the expressive quality of phonemes, which becomes evident in poetry, I want to draw attention to the fact that syllables are like colors and that both syllables and colors are useful as references to certain aspects of spiritual reality, or the sacred.

Now consider the components of the mantra Om Mani Padme Hum.

We have already seen that the Om refers to the whole, but also the Hum is a universal mantram.

And just as the Om is at the beginning of many mantras, we find the Hum at the end of many of them, as their closure.

We may say that if the Om evokes the all, Hum alludes to the nothing, for Hum is something like the extract of the all, its quintessence.

It can be said that this Hum (and also the Hu, through which God is evoked in the Sufi tradition) is the sound closest to Buddhahood— the transcendent emptiness in all.

I invite you now to savor what the sonority of the "H" in this mantram communicates, this voiceless consonant, the sound of which is nothing but breathing.

Does this not lend itself to making a reference to the invisible?

We find a similar meaning of the "H" in the Hebrew language. In the Old Testament it is explained that at some point in his life Abram received the name of Abraham from God.

The addition of this "H" to his name conveys the idea of a spiritual insufflation that we might compare to God, according to the same book of Genesis, breathing life into Adam.

But why Hum and not Ham or Hem?
And why Hu and not Hi?

I invite you to explore the colors associated with the vowels, beginning with the A, which suggests the white light that has not been broken into the colors of the rainbow.
And now compare it with the Ooooooooooo, of Om...
As we have seen, Om evokes the whole, just as its circular shape does. But UUUUUUU is different ...
How can we describe it?
Does it evoke a particular color?
Indeed it does, blue. If A is white and O is black, U is blue.
What else do we feel by singing it?
Yes, depth. It seems to want to lead us to an increasing depth, as if we have slipped down a tuuuuuuuube. Let's try to exaggerate what it evokes in us when we sing it, so that we become clearer: uuuuuuuuuu ...

Would you not say that it invites us to something like ecstasy? Something like a great pleasure that is associated with the unlimited, the immensity, the open, space ...
Let's now explore the final "I" in Mani.

Mani means "jewel," but the presence of the letter "I" gives it a particularly luminous character, brighter than white.

And among all colors, is there one brighter than white?

Yellow, that we associate with the sun, but also with certain flowers, and wheat fields, and certain butterflies and precious stones.

The "A" in Mani is on the first syllable of Padme, which you probably already know. It literally means "lotus" and is an image equivalent to the rose of the Christian world. Like the rose, the lotus is a symbol of love, but also of life and spiritual growth.

Sometimes the mantra is translated as "the jewel in the lotus," which seems to have no obvious meaning, even though you can sometimes see a jewel at the center of a lotus, but in the Vajrayana tradition both symbols put together also convey a sexual meaning, so that the jewel represents the male and the lotus the female.

But this complementarity can be also understood as a contrast between two forms of love, Mani being love's concentration on something very small (like the care that a jeweler puts in the making of a jewel) and Padma a form of love that is like an expansive movement of distribution or dissemination.

We can say that there is a "masculine" feeling that searches for the great, the sublime, the vast or the titanic, and another "feminine" feeling that pays more attention to what is lacking, much like a mother who cares more for the child that is most needy.

After this general introduction to mantric chanting, let us proceed to a chant, but for today I will invite you to an act of empathic listening rather than chanting with your own voice—an experience in which you identify with the experience of those who are chanting. I will use a recording of Tibetan monks with Yungchen Lhamo, and I recommend you make their voices into your own prayer asking for a greater capacity for compassion.

When you find recordings of Tibetan music that have become commercially available, the spirit of this music is not that of performance, as in Western music, but ritual, the purpose of which is more spiritual than aesthetic.

Thus, the guttural throat voices singing the Mani on this recording are not generated by performers but by monks, for whom singing is inseparable from their practice.

And when the one who practices is someone who has spent many years involved in the spirit of his practice (as in the case of monks truly intending to generate compassion in themselves), such singing becomes potentially infectious.

Particularly if we make it our own, and imagine that we are asking, through their voices, to increase our capacity for love.

We will listen with closed eyes (even though we are sitting face-to-face) and then move on to our silent meditation, but first let me say a bit more about what you are about to hear.

First, a group of monks recites the mantra in a deep voice, and during this part I suggest that you identify with their chanting, not as one who feigns compassion that he does not feel, but as one who is eager to come to feel it, as if praying, "May I become compassionate."

Then you hear the voice of a woman, who also sings Om Mani Padme Hum, only much more slowly, extending each syllable through several notes, on another scale of time and with great sweetness.

And if you imagine singing with the monks from your Hara, it would seem that this high, sweet voice comes from above you, as if it were pouring over your head like golden honey.

It is as if, when you are asking for compassion, it comes to you, embodied musically in Yungchen Lhamo's singing.

It will be brief, but I imagine it is enough to bring new inspiration into your silent meditation.

Then we'll practice once again an awareness of the here and now, while trying to look from an identification with space and adopting the view that everything there is exists in a vastness which is con-sciousness itself—just with fewer words on my part, which will also allow you to get used to it without my instructions.

(Recording)

And now we return to Vipassana from the perspective of space.

We now begin to open our eyes and, using the stimulus of external space to evoke a space as immense as possible, we also identify our minds with space.
Let the body sink to the ground,
so that it feels as heavy as a mountain,
but let your mind dissolve into space with weightless levity.

Feel how space helps you relax,
not only physically.
It is as if you could surrender to space all the heaviness,

the stress, and even your Karma.
From our habitual perspective, it would seem that we need to
invent space as we imagine it, but in reality, it is what most
resembles our fundamental reality.
So we can even adopt the point of view that all that exists is like a
creation of space.

We can experiment with this way of seeing things.
We may adopt the view that in reality there is nothing,
and that our ordinary reality is constructed.
And when that point of view is achieved,
it leads to a great relief, and great fluidity.

Let us try to discern whether beyond the consciousness of so many
things, such as tactile consciousness, emotional consciousness,
consciousness of thoughts, all sorts of mental phenomena,
there is also pure consciousness,
an awareness of consciousness itself,
a consciousness that is pure presence,
and try to focus on it.

Conceive of all mental phenomena as existing in something like a
sponge of pure consciousness.
And now let us continue
but in contact through the gaze,
so as to give an opportunity for mind-contagion.

Dropping all effort,
much as when surrendering the body to gravity
and allowing the mind to evaporate in space.
When everything falls or is dissolved, what remains?

Let us identify with what in ourselves is always still.

For consciousness itself is quiet,
even though everything in it moves spontaneously.

And let us allow ourselves not to be interested in what moves,
but just in our stillness.
And to whoever is tired, I suggest you close your eyes and see how
much more you can rest, yet in the same position,
renouncing any effort.

6

Time and the Eternal Present

As we have seen, a big key in Tibetan Buddhism is space, and there are several tantras about space. But today we will consider another key element, which is time.

Let us begin with something we already know: concentrating in the present.

It is something that is talked about a lot today, because the "here and now" is on everyone's lips, and not only in the context of Buddhist meditation.

(Soon a congress of education will take place in Spain, for example, that is being advertised as "educating ourselves in the now").

I have already commented on how, if we are serious about regarding the past as already past, this may be enough to dispel some of our worrying.

And if we think that not only the past is gone, but also that the future doesn't yet exist, this can bring our present experience into focus. But that is not the case in our every day experience, as is reflected when we talk and say very little about the now.

We speak of the past and we speak about the future; we share plans, expectations, anticipations, but we find it difficult to talk about the "now" because the now is always a little too intimate, and even if "nothing happens," we want to make a big secret about nothing happening. Perhaps we consider ourselves very interesting, and it seems inconsistent with this to confess that "we are just here" and have nothing more to say. Maybe we feel that it is proof of an unmentionable mediocrity?

Even though the personal influence of Fritz Perls and the title of Ram Dass' book *Be Here Now* made the philosophy of living in the present somewhat fashionable in the Sixties, it is also true that— despite this (and also despite the existentialists)—few are living in the present, and also few communicate what is happening to them.

But what Mahayana Buddhism states is that, apart from the future not yet existing and the past having passed, it is also the case that if we look carefully at the now (especially if we look at a brief enough present moment) it is likely that we will not find anything there.

For thoughts are rather slow, and if we want to translate our present into verbal thinking (as if we were talking to ourselves), this is more than can fit into an instant.

It might seem too incredible that not only do the future and the past not exist, but neither does the present; but if you want to refer back to the experience of the present, it happens that in the infinitesimal instant you can just find yourself with yourself.

Just as we can sharpen the focus of a flashlight to shine its light in a precise spot, we may also do something similar with our attention, and what do we find in an instant so brief that there is no time for thinking?

Could it be that in this instant where thoughts disappear we could find ourselves with our own mind?

We know we are there, waiting, or looking for something.

Perhaps we find ourselves there, or perhaps we don't. But the usual experience is that when we look for the hidden treasure at the heart of our existence, we seem to not find anything ... just as it happened when we observed our mind at rest.

However, as in that case, it is possible that our "*not* finding anything" will become a "*finding* nothing": finding our invisible presence, which is a pure look, a pure subject, which is represented in Buddhist iconography as a naked blue Buddha.

But let us now go into the corresponding practice.

Please pair up with someone and I will be going over some of the things you already heard me explain in the context of a guided meditation.

Since we are perhaps not completely convinced that there is no past, it is not a bad idea to renounce it.

And let's give up the future too.

And if we now give up thinking, now that we have some practice in remaining inwardly silent, we will have nothing besides being present without words.
We already know this experience.

Ordinarily the experience of the present is always a little different, like Heraclitus' famous river, since we are in a world of changing sounds and, at the same time, in a world of bodily sensations and in a world that has an emotional atmosphere. But if we silence our thinking or if we circumscribe our attention to the fleeting present, trying to capture the moment, we will surely be left with what appears to be nothing. Let's savor that.

And instead of considering our not perceiving anything as a failure, let us consider it an achievement; that is, as a technique to go beyond thought and beyond "the ten thousand things."

Sometimes I have compared meditation to what happens in a dark room in which one cannot see anything yet one knows that one is there. In a dark room your sense of presence comes from feeling your body and being in contact with your breath—so that you must rely on stimuli beyond the merely visual. When you find nothing in your quiet mind, however, your knowing that you are present is not dependent on external stimuli and needs to be more subtle. Yet one does not have a fine enough attention to detect that "one is there."

Your meditation, then, while attending to the instant, will consist in knowing that *you are there although this cannot be ascertained from sensations.*

Our usual condition is that of not feeling ourselves, but we may understand that focusing on the instantaneous now involves an opportunity to "be there" in the apparent nothing.

If we come to it, we will have come to what is called in Buddhism "intrinsic awareness," which is so familiar to us that we cannot ordinarily detect it, much as it is said that fish are not aware of the water in which they move.

Yet if we fail to see in ourselves that "original face before our parents were born" and miss the essence of the mind that we seek, we are to just stay there, in the not finding anything. Being there where there is nothing constitutes an unusual state, different from our daily lives, and simply familiarizing ourselves with such "consciousness without an object" is like watering a plant that has the potential for growth.

Meditating, then, is not just waiting for that invisible subject of consciousness to appear, but is also familiarizing oneself with that state of being where there is nothing. Sometimes you cannot stay there more than a couple of seconds, and the work will consist of coming to be able to stay longer and longer.

But now let us relax again the focus of our attention, letting in what comes from the peripheral field, remembering that we have a body, that we are sitting, that there are sounds, and come back to the field of the ordinary here and now where there are all kinds of stimuli.

7

On Devotion and Guru Rinpoche's Mantram

I have said that Tibetan Buddhism integrates the practices of Shamata and Vipassana but is particularly interested in understanding the mind beyond mental phenomena.

We become interested in what we may call the "deep mind," which also coincides with the deep truth of the philosophers and is not a matter of thinking but of a possible experience.

And we have seen that the development of compassion is highly recommended as indispensable to those who aspire to this goal.

But I have explained that the Vajrayana not only emphasizes compassion—but also devotion—and may be called a religion no less devotional than Christianity, Hinduism, or Islam.

In the Christian tradition, which is a continuation of Judaism, we know that the First Commandment is to love God.

Thus, in the Judeo-Christian view of life, the most important of all precepts is the one that reads: "You shall love God with all your heart and with all your strength."

And it is also said in the Christian tradition, which emphasizes love of neighbor and self, that we should "love God above all things."

But we are far from such conviction in our present secular society, so that for many it has come to seem doubtful that we need to love a God who perhaps does not exist.

And we've certainly come to our secular culture after a long period of confusion between genuine devotion and a hypocritical parody of it that has arisen from an authoritarian mandate.

I would not say that this phenomenon has arisen in India, where devotion continues to be a way to access the experience of the divine—a yoga which can enable even a person of little yogic training to get very far.

And that's one of the characteristics of devotion: that when it is deep and sincere, the seeker can skip much of the way. It is as if the higher world or a cosmic intelligence responds to people animated by a strong motivation of the right kind.

This devotional element is very present in Tibetan Buddhism, as anyone who has had contact with the Tibetans has surely felt. I have had occasion to walk with a group of Tibetan pilgrims chanting mantras, and my feeling was like being in the middle of a beehive, perhaps because I have always associated the buzzing of bees with an intense dedication.

The emotional intensity of mantra chanting can make Tibetan prayer also reminiscent of the purr of a cat, that not only seems very intimate, but also tender. But just as the love of God can manifest itself in ways that we do not recognize as "love of God," devotion is more than what we *call* devotion.

Such that working on oneself towards the improvement of one's mind is not just discipline but an act of love for something deep inside ourselves and the expression of a longing for a fulfillment that we feel we can achieve.

So that we may ask: is the object of our longing toward the realization of what we call "our potential" something different from the divine?

Yet in spite of such implicit devotion, we sometimes forget that we are caring for ourselves, because we are so imprisoned by our super-egoic functioning that what we have decided to do becomes an obligation which we may then rebel against.

One says to oneself, for example, "I will meditate," then no longer wants to meditate in rebellion to such an order. It is therefore appropriate to remember our most valid motivation, which is not that of disciplining ourselves but that of love towards our ideal and of charity towards our underdeveloped and suffering being.

It's convenient, in other words, to remind yourself, "This is good for you," or maybe, "Remember that this serves you and will empower you to be of service."

Aside from the Bodhisattva vow, which is an affirmation of the purpose of working to cleanse one's mind to serve—and constitutes a very loving vow in which compassion and devotion converge—loving one's neighbor is also regarded as an imitation of God in the Judeo-Christian tradition.

Another devotional act formalized in Buddhist practice is what is called Refuge. Already early Buddhism includes a ceremonial Refuge that consists of a series of three bows in which this formula is repeated:

I take refuge in the Buddha.
I take refuge in the Dharma.
I take refuge in the Sangha.

where Buddha, Dharma and Sangha are understood in varying degrees of depth.

The Buddha was originally the teacher Siddhartha Gautama—the historical Buddha was originally considered a human being who came to full enlightenment and then, in the Mahayana period, was conceived as a being of cosmic proportions who has always existed and can directly help his devotees.

In the Vajrayana period, not only did the devotion to the Buddha further increase, but extended to many beings of divine stature that are sometimes called "Buddhas," though more precisely qualified as Bodhisattvas, protectors, *dakinis,* or fairies.

In addition, substantial respect for living Buddhas results in a much greater respect for teachers than that inspired in their disciples by Theravada or even Ch'an (or Zen) instructors—to say nothing of the respect shown in the Western traditions to priests or church dignitaries who, even in the times of St. Augustine during the fourth century, were sometimes elected because they had a good voice or gave eloquent sermons, and have since continued to come to their positions through patience, political influence, and even money.

In contrast to what the history of the church tells us regarding the non-spiritual factors that determine that someone can become a Pope, in Zen Buddhism whoever is recognized as a teacher must have given proof of his spiritual realization, not just by passing the "Satori test" given by their expert teacher, but having matured through many moments of Satori.

In a good Zen school, Satori (i.e., understanding the essence of Buddhahood) can be reached in about three years, but the integration of such realization into ordinary life may be achieved only after twenty years or so.

Moreover, in the case of the Tibetan tradition, the training of lamas or teachers has usually involved not only great dedication and a very deep knowledge, but also the development of shamanic powers. Since it is very difficult in the Western world for lamas to continue to be trained as they were before the Chinese invasion of Tibet, we do not know what the future of this tradition may be.

But even if devotional practices abound in Tibetan Buddhism that involve the invocation or identification with such entities as we can see represented in many pieces of sacred art and that may be described as "angels" or "tutelary deities" (such as the Bodhisattvas of compassion, knowledge and power, or other entities that expert teachers know to assign to their disciples according to their personality), nothing is as important in this tradition as the devotion to one's own teacher, sometimes practiced in a formal way through Guru Yoga and at other times simply through an attitude of receptivity and surrender that arises from the recognition of an enlightened mind, which makes the devotee receptive to his blessings.

It is because of such blessings that we can say that Tibetan Buddhism is *magical*.

While for us Westerners, if someone asks his father: "Do I have your blessing on my project?," this means nothing more than getting acceptance or permission, in the spiritual world blessings are a much more real thing, that we could compare to the blind Isaac of the Old Testament, who blesses Jacob when he takes the place of his hairy elder brother.

According to that story, although Isaac comes to realize that he was duped, he can no longer withdraw his blessing, which constituted an irreversible act.

I think we have enough information from various cultures to understand that both blessings and curses are real—as are white magicians and black magicians—and both have existed throughout Tibetan history, as befits the fact that Tantric Buddhism was established in "the land of snows" by a teacher who was also known as a great magician.

I tell this as a preface to devotion felt by Tibetans toward a teacher who, in the history of Tibetan Buddhism, has been likened to a second Buddha—Padmasambhava, also known as Guru Rinpoche or the Precious Guru, who is said to have been born only eight years after Buddha's Parinirvana, yet is known for bringing tantric teachings to Tibet in the eighth century.

Padmasambhava means "born from the lotus" and the legend of his birth strikes us as far more miraculous than other virgin births. There are many virgin births in world history: Jesus Christ, the Buddha, Lao Tse (who according to legend was born from the side of his mother), and Krishna (Such legends have been believed literally, as in ancient cultures, in which history is imbued with mythical content and legends are an attempt to convey symbolic truths that have been considered of greater significance than the simple facts of the past).

But in the legend of Padmasambhava the emphasis on the symbolic level seems even more striking, the fact that he has not had worldly parents suggesting that our deepest nature is not born from our mother or father.

There is a biography of Padmasambhava and every step in it is as amazing as his birth, so we might believe that the great teacher was only a mythical being. Yet there is no doubt that he lived in the eighth century, which is not so far back, and that he came to Tibet after King Trisong Detsen had already tried to bring Buddhism into his country through Shantarakshita and Vimalamitra.

Due to the opposition of the former religion of the Bonpos, the attempt had not succeeded, and it is said that Padmasambhava triumphed by converting the divinities of the Bonpos to Buddhism through his great magical power.

Not only is Guru Rinpoche a teacher of teachers and a powerful wizard for the Tibetans, but a figure comparable to the Virgin Mary for having appeared most frequently to his Tibetan devotees.

(Shortly after I met my own root teacher, Tarthang Tulku Rinpoche, one of his first instructions was: "Pray much to Padmasambhava, with tears in your eyes, so that he may show himself to you." And though he never made a physical apparition or even a vision, I have at times felt that I have received his blessings).

In a representation of Padmasambhava, he is represented with a Vajra, the ritual instrument symbolizing both the diamond and lightning, but also the indestructible core of our existence—beyond thinking, feeling, and willing.

What is it that lies beyond the wanting, feeling, and thinking?

We might say nothing, yet we may also employ the Buddhist concept of "the un-originated," which points to what transcends the world of matter-energy in time and space.

Everything in life is in flux or, as it is said most often in Buddhism, everything is "impermanent"—except consciousness itself which, like the empty field that contains all things, is also like the diamond, known not only for its transparency and luminosity, but also as the hardest material in nature (In industry, for example, the diamond is used for cutting steel).

The main form of devotional practice toward Padmasambhava is the mantra through which he is invoked—usually called the "Vajra Guru Mantra," which I will explain below.

It begins with the **Om, A, Hum** syllables—which you may have already known as an independent mantra—alluding to the triad of body, speech, and mind, and also to the chakras that are particularly associated with these three aspects of our existence. It then continues with **Vajra Guru Padma Siddhi** and finally, like many complex mantras, it ends with **Hum**.

We can conceive of the series of Vajra Guru Padma Siddhi and Hum (that follow the initial OM AH HUM) as a mandala constituted of five elements, with the final Hum at the center—a mandala representing the five Buddha families, so that we may say that one meaning of the mantra is the evocation of Padmasambhava as a synthesis of the Enlightened qualities of all the Buddhas of all times.

I have already explained, in reference to the mantra of the Bodhisattva of compassion—Chenrezig, or Avalokiteshvara—the meanings of Hum and Padme and I have also said something about the Vajra or scepter (that Tibetans pronounce Benza), but there are two more terms that need to be explained.

In this context of this mantram, GURU refers to Padmasambhava himself, of course, so that VAJRA GURU can be translated as the Guru that wields the vajra. It is also a term referring to the inner guidance that is a part of everyone's mind, of which the external master is a reflection and an intermediary.

Siddhi refers to the powers of the Siddhas—those who have reached their fullness after traveling all phases of the path—among which there is a distinction between ordinary powers such as clairvoyance or bi-location and the extraordinary power of transmitting Enlightenment. It has often been pointed out that the development of these powers constitutes a danger to one's spiritual progress, yet it is important to know that they are characteristic of the Siddhas or great masters, just as they are characteristic of Christian saints.

Having already explained the components of "the mantra of the twelve syllables," as it is sometimes called, I invite you to listen to it through a recording distributed by the Rigpa Foundation in which Lama Sogyal chants with a group of disciples.

Take it as an opportunity for empathetic listening—that is, take their invocation of the blessings of the precious Guru as your own. Immediately after this, and without any further words, we will return to the practice of "Vipassana from the perspective of space."

8

The Awareness of a Subtle Body

The practical knowledge of those physical phenomena—which are sometimes mentioned in transpersonal psychology as "energy" and "energy centers" and that in Hindu culture (also among the Sikhs) are called Kundalini Yoga—has reached a high degree of development in Tibetan Buddhism, giving rise to the specialty called Za-Lung, in reference to the Nadis or subtle channels (Za) and air or Prana (Lung) flowing through them.

There has been very little access by Westerners to what the Tibetan tradition teaches concerning the body, in part likely because it is believed that the movement of subtle energies is activated spontaneously by deep meditation.

It will certainly not be unfamiliar to those who, during meditation, experience physical phenomena such as their heart and forehead opening or eyes turning back toward the center of their forehead.

Streams of energy may also be felt in one's body such as those described by practitioners of body therapies (and particularly those familiar with Reichian or Neoreichian therapy from which "bioenergetics" has arisen). Following Stanislav Grof's suggestion, talk about "pranic phenomena" has entered the therapeutic world.

There are many sensations that are associated with both meditation and with the effects of psychedelic drugs and, more accurately speaking, not just sensations but subtle physiological phenomena, little known to modern science.

Traditionally, it used to be said (although it does not seem scientifically correct to me) that the *Nadis* or subtle Prana channels exist in the body but they have never been found in our anatomy. Personal experience tells me that the phenomenon that underlies the sensations of Prana flow is a pulsation of muscle fibers and muscle bundles that takes place during the relaxation that comes with a deep surrender.

Whoever feels it (and because I have lived it for decades I've observed it a lot) can also perceive that the movement of Prana progresses through the body in time—as though through a labyrinth—and the body is no longer controlled by the inhibitory pyramidal system (involved in Reich's "character armor," which can be considered intrinsic to the usual ego).

It begins to become like a pulsating anemone or like a fish, in which we can see wave-like movements going from the nose or mouth toward the tail.

Whoever can let go sufficiently of the chronic muscle tone that is like a physical echo of our compulsive attitude to life also comes to discover, at least for a moment, this internal pulsating movement, and sometimes a flow that goes from head to toe that is already well known in the Theravada tradition.

And have some of you not felt during meditation something like a cloak falling on you from above? Or perhaps you may have felt a shower of "energy" on you—as in the myth of Daphne, who is inseminated by Zeus in the form of a golden rain.

Some have interpreted such sensations as a mantle of grace or as a descending spiritual energy. But the beginning can be very physical, as in Sri Aurobindo's Yoga, in which it is recommended that we pay special attention to a pressure on the top of the head, attributed to the "force" that wants to penetrate our body from above.

It is, then, a natural phenomenon but a little known one and there are not very many who reach a level of meditation in which the body loosens up sufficiently to begin a process of transformation that is like an incubation of an "energy body" (called an "etheric" body in theosophy). Special practices may be added to this natural process of transformation, among which the best known and most important is the first of "Naropa's yogas," called Tumo or "inner heat."

But a presentation of Tumo would not be appropriate as part of this brief introduction to Tibetan Buddhism given to a group that includes some who have not even established a regular meditation practice. (Also, much as it served me very much some decades ago, I do not feel I have enough experience to teach it). But there are certain things that I think are relevant and interesting for everyone to sample and I want to dedicate the rest of this morning to those.

Firstly, I would like to invite you to focus on that center that the Japanese call Hara and the Chinese the Dantien (or lower cauldron) which is located a little below the navel and a couple of fingers' width behind the abdominal wall.

When you passed through the SAT (Seekers After Truth) program, I recommended that you cultivate the ongoing awareness of the Hara through ordinary life, and also that you read Durkheim's book of the same name (*Hara*). Next, I proposed that you meditate with a focus on the Hara during the time we dedicated to Zazen. I also explained how Hakuin was able to heal his "Zen disease" after incorporating into his practice this aspect of the Taoist tradition, which he later bequeathed not only to his disciples but, indirectly, to all presently surviving Zen lineages.

If you persist in the practice of visualizing the Hara and also try to *feel* it, you may come to develop a felt sense that there is something there. One way to make that happen is by visualizing fire, and trying to feel your Hara heating up. We will do that right now and will rely on the use of a mantram: RAM, which precisely evokes fire.

You may chant with the voice or intonation that you want, without all necessarily doing it at the same time, and we fill the space with the sound of Ram, taking the sound and the feel of the RRRRR—evocative of an engine—so as to increase our evocation of fire. We chant as if wanting to light a fire with the mantra, while trying to feel heat in our lower abdomen.

This area is like the root of the chakras. For even though there are chakras below the Hara, it is as if this root supplies what is above, which is what we work the most. Thus we may think about what we are about to do as recharging the energy of the entire vertical chakra system.

Ram, Ram, Ram, Ram ...

Now let's chant Om, feeling it resonate in the center of our head. And let us visualize a white Om in our head, even though the sound of O is rather dark.

And let us also seek to visualize white light radiating from the OM in our head.

Om, Om, Om ...

Now I suggest you position yourself in front of someone, so that what we do next serves as preliminary to our usual meditation.

The starting point prior to bodily visualizations related to the chakras is leaving behind the ordinary, everyday body, and to do this we imagine our body as transparent.
This is in itself a powerful exercise, which may go a long way.

Let us then imagine our body as transparent. Or perhaps as a soap bubble, with only a vaguely visible outline.

I don't know if any one of you has seen one of those crystal skulls that have been found in the ruins of Mexican temples. They suggest that the ancient Mexicans may have known this transparent body experience, since a transparent head is an especially important aspect of the experience—making the bones of the face and skull actually *feel* transparent. Also, the hands are difficult, perhaps because there is so much pent-up tension in them. Let us then visualize our hands as becoming transparent, and also feel we have transparent feet.

Perhaps you have already perceived the effect of this practice, which might seem to be simply a visualization but has a physical effect. For when we make our body transparent, it seems to become more permeable, and this permeability promotes the energy-flow.

And our psyche also becomes more transparent, in a way similar to what happens when we visualize it as existing in space. Just like evoking the permeability of space is enough for the body to open, when one opens one's body, making it transparent, it feels as if it has merged with space.

And now I invite you to visualize a vertical central axis at the center of our transparent body. We already have a sense of having something like a pillar that goes through us since we are vertebrates, but the central axis that we visualize in Buddhist practice is not exactly the spine, but a more central axis that does not exist anatomically.

Imagine a clear blue axis from the crown of the head to the perineum, at the base of the trunk. And visualize it as an *empty* central axis, of a blue color that we associate with the sky, and with space.

We visualize, then, a transparent blue tube (called the Uma) as the central axis of our transparent body.

This way of feeling the body as organized around an empty center corresponds with the Buddhist analysis of the experienced body, represented by a series of Mandalas, each with an empty center that may be understood as a reference to the emptiness of the mind itself, at the core of our field of experience.

Beyond the specific domains of our experience, the essence of our consciousness is intangible, and the central channel—or Uma—echoes the fact that we are tangible and visible only at the periphery of ourselves, while we remain empty in the middle.

And now let us turn to another aspect of what is sometimes called the "subtle body," which manifests in the form of sensations that go beyond simple visualization, and are part of the subtle physiology of advanced meditation.

Apart from the central channel that meditation helps us discover but is part of our structure, there are also two "lateral channels" that somehow represent our experience of asymmetrical bilateralism.

For we are not perfectly symmetrical; we have a qualitative difference between left and right. Already in the ancient yoga tradition, a qualitative difference is described between our left and right as a contrast between the sun and the moon, one side being more active and the other more sensitive and receptive.

If we try to visualize and feel to the left and right of the Uma, these two other channels—a red one on the right and a white one on the left—we might find it is much easier said than done, because body visualizations are not quite independent from the physical experience, and there are opaque body regions: channels that have not yet opened as part of our psycho-spiritual development.

Seeking to visualize these three channels that run through our body from our nostrils to the Hara is said to facilitate their eventual opening, however, and also serves as preliminary to the visualization of the chakras. I will not describe more precisely for now the "subtle anatomy" of the channels aside from explaining that they intersect between our eyebrows (as do the nerve pathways from our cerebral hemispheres) and that they join the central channel at the Hara.

But now we will proceed to visualize a Buddha in our heart. Let us first begin with the Hum sound, but now only as an imagined sound and the color blue.

Imagine that a blue shape is forming from the central channel— a blue form that begins to take the form of a Buddha.

Visualizations usually involve many details, so that visualizing many things simultaneously involves a splitting of our focus. We can say, among other things, that visualizations, aside from a devotional aspect, are exercises in the simultaneous attention to different elements.

But these elements in a visualization also transmit certain meanings like, for example, the representation of Buddha as always sitting on a lotus.

Let's visualize a white lotus in our hearts, flourishing and radiant, and over it let us visualize the blue Buddha. I am simplifying because in the traditional practice a schematic sun and a moon are also imagined over this lotus, but for now let us simply proceed to the most important thing, which is to feel the blue Buddha in our heart.

I say "feel" rather than "imagine" or "visualize" for if the Buddha is a representation of the divine background of consciousness within each of us, feeling a Buddha in the heart is to feel something sacred within us—thus feeling that we carry within us a very precious treasure.

And what treasure is bigger than the mysterious depth of consciousness itself, at the bottom of what we call merely human? If we regard consciousness as the basis out of which all other experiences and things are derived, including love, visualizing the Buddha within us should be a sacred endeavor and also open us to Buddha's blessing.

We visualize a sitting Buddha in a meditation position, with his hands together at the center, as in Zen Buddhism, and surrounded by a pink halo.

And the blue Buddha holds something very precious in his heart, that we can visualize as a white pearl. And within that precious pearl we imagine the sound "Broom," manifesting as the light blue of electric sparks. And we stay with this for a while because this visualization has an effect on the energy body, which feels as if it has compensated somewhat for the narrowness of our heart,the armoring of our loving capacity.

Finally, I invite you to imagine that our visualization merges into our own body. The Buddha fades and merges with our own body in all directions, yet leaving us with the feeling of having a sacred heart, even if we forget about it in our daily experience.

But as we dissolve the Buddha that we visualized in our hearts, imagine that his holiness fills the rest of our body, and imagine what it might be like to have a Buddha body.
A sanctified body that might radiate blessings.

But this exercise in visualization has probably fatigued our attention by now. Perhaps it is time that we return to rest, only without changing our posture.

We remain in the same position without trying to do anything, just being open to whatever happens.

In Buddhism, being the receptivity to what happens is called our "Buddha nature," which is like the space through which what happens happens, or the mirror that reflects what is.

The better we meditate, the more restful the meditation should be.

We just let everything be as it is, even if it hurts, for it is likely that we have Karma to burn, or experiences to digest, and then meditation becomes a space for such digestion.

And just as in Christian mythology it is said that souls in purgatory are happy as they undergo a painful purification process, for they know that they are headed to Heaven, there is in meditation a suffering compatible with a basically happy state, just as many times we smile even at things that bother us.

Not with a fake smile, but with something like affection for ourselves. Now let us open our eyes and keep on doing what we are doing in front of the person we are facing, while we allow ourselves to be transparent to another. With no other purpose than to be there, perceiving what happens and especially perceiving ourselves as the field in which everything happens.

[Gong]

Addendum

As an addition to the above-described series of meditations I now add—under the headline of "contemplations of death"—a series of exercises that I have devised and which, despite their coherence with the spirit of Tibetan Buddhism, cannot exactly be presented as part of the tradition. This may also be said concerning the last meditation which, though I have borrowed it from Eckhart Tolle, results in an experience comparable to that of Vipassana from the perspective of space.

Contemplations of Death

I have already presented to you many ways of meditating; however, in Eastern traditions meditation is presented within a context, and the work that I propose, too, dwells in a context that involves such things as healing our relationships with others through the development of a loving attitude.

In Buddhism though, not only a context of understanding and virtue is regarded as important, and the Tibetan tradition proposes a series of preliminary practices that includes keeping in mind our mortality.

We may think that we are already quite aware of this, but it is not completely true that we know it, for sometimes we know it and at other times we forget it—so it would be truer to say that we only half know it.

In one of his books, Idries Shah recounts an anecdote of Uways Al-Qarni, a contemporary of Muhammad who is considered one of the first Sufis. To someone who has asked him, "How do you feel?," he replies, "Like one who is going to die."

"But we all feel like that!," answered his questioner, to which Al-Qarni replied in turn: "Yes, it happens to us all. But who *feels* it?

Gurdjieff says that we are more afraid of finding a mouse in our bed than of the fact that we are going to die.

It is only intellectually that we know we are going to die, for we have seemingly protected ourselves from feeling the ephemeral nature of our existence, which would surely lead us in turn to feel that our lives are meaningless.

Yet, is it not true that some people who have been close to death go through a transformation? So say those who have researched the experiences that Americans have called NDE: "Near Death Experiences."

For my part, I believe that there is nothing more important in meditation than deciding to die.

This may happen to one who has sufficiently observed one's mind and has seen clearly how it produces incessant, insubstantial, and idle thoughts, much as one in a carousel constantly pursues the next moment and the next thought, going from desire to desire.

Such a person may then come to wonder about the point of all of this. It is from disenchantment with one's own "monkey mind" that there may arise a willingness to give up such an interest in the worldly mind and thus become able to access a higher realm of consciousness.

We know that the process of enlightenment entails an "annihilation" of ordinary consciousness, but it seems we do not know this well enough to surrender ourselves, and we cling to ourselves as one who has not become sufficiently disenchanted with the "Samsaric mind."

We are still hopeful that, just around the corner, we will find a fundamental thought or the fulfillment of this or that other desire.

As such, an aspect of the experience of meditation is a process of disenchantment, through which we learn to let go of our greed in order to become disinterested in the ephemeral and thus capable of equanimity.

I

Many years ago, I came across a very interesting proposal in a study of values. An American social psychologist I met named Hadley Cantril gave me a values survey to read in the early 1960s and in it, he had used an imaginary letter: Someone tells a friend that he has gone to the doctor, who has found gastric cancer, and now he knows that he only has about 6 months to live.

Cantril used this imaginary letter to ask his experimental subjects straight off: What would you do with your life if you only had six months left?

One of Akira Kurosawa's old films—still black-and-white—called *To Live*, presents the story of someone who experienced something similar.

The main protagonist is a bored official working in a Japanese governmental office who, up until now, seems to have lived with no further purpose other than to serve an obstructive bureaucracy.

A community group requests that a certain plot of land be transformed into a children's park, but he routinely says "no," and "processes" them—sending them, for example to office number 45, where they will later be sent elsewhere.

Following a routine visit to his doctor where this official learns that he has a limited time left to live, he wants, for the first time, to find meaning in his life and begins to do new things, like choosing to talk to people.

For example, when he sees a girl full of vitality, he wonders, "What could the secret of her joy be?" There comes a time when he realizes that it is in the very public office where he has worked until now where he could do something worth-while. The project of a park for the children that so far had been rejected begins to make sense to him as something that could be useful, and he ends up becoming a hero for his support of a good cause, even though until then he had only been a defender of the status quo.

I have summarized the argument of this film to propose to you now that you imagine yourselves in the situation of the main character.

That is to say: imagine that through a routine medical examina-tion, you are shocked to discover that you will only have six more months to live.

I ask you, as my friend Cantril inquired in his study about values, what would your priorities be during this limited time?

Cantril asked that question with an interest in knowing the values of a social group, while I am asking it to help you become aware of issues that you are putting off—matters that we continue to postpone in view of the assumption that there will be time for them in the future, but which in the face of considering a life with a very limited future, will claim their urgency.

The question I ask you, then, is: If you saw yourselves in the situ-ation described, what would your priorities be?

It is clear that when one realizes that one is impermanent, one becomes more interested in and begins to give priority to the inner work. Instead of saying to oneself that one will meditate later, when this or that is resolved, one who already understands the path will want to prepare for the precious opportunity that death entails to meet a higher Truth.

For one who has had the taste of this contemplation, it may make sense to cultivate the daily reminder that one day he or she will die (as well as all of our acquaintances), and this will serve as a stimulus to keep alive the motivation to take advantage of every moment of life in the development of consciousness.

II

However, now I would like to invite you to another experiment—
similar to the one we have shared, only with a different time
frame. What would the priorities be if we had only two months to
live? Clearly there are many things that one can set out to do in
six months—such as completing unfinished projects or resolving
unsettled situations with this or that other person. However, when
we only have two months, there will be no time for such matters;
we will discover other priorities and surely discovering them will
serve our present life.

I now propose a few minutes of silence, and then we will share.

.....

I hope that this time the things that you have felt are priorities,
whether asking for forgiveness or forgiving, enjoying life and
friendship or distancing oneself from social life, and meditating or
simply doing nothing—become, after this reflection, more present
in your lives.

Now I invite you to an imaginary anticipation, seemingly similar
and at the same time very different: to imagine that we have only
ten minutes to live.

One way of doing this could be to imagine that news has reached us
that a missile has been fired, perhaps by mistake, and that we know
that very soon it will fall on us with a fatal explosive charge.

What stirs in us —or what do we do—by imagining that we have
such a short time left?

Generally, the effect of such an anticipation is that it induces in us something like a spontaneous meditation—a going within to our own center, or an invocation of divinity or an attitude of surrender.

As Tótila Albert said:

To that wisdom may we come:
Knowing how to surrender
Our empty soul.

Let it be an inspiration to us now—as we imagine that we are doomed to a death without appeal in a few minutes.

III

Although just imagining that one has little time to live is enough to feel called to one's own center, let us now take a step further in the contemplation of death—imagining ourselves dead. That is to say, exploring the experience of death here and now—not the agony of one dying but the condition of one who has died, which is to have lost the body, the senses, the emotions, and the faculties of thinking or imagining. I invite you, then, to "die before you die."

For this, we will take some time to change positions, lying down on the floor. If you wish, you can adopt the position of the corpse of yoga: with your back flat against the floor, your arms at your sides, and your palms facing up.

And now imagine yourselves dead.

I am not inviting you to imagine yourselves as ghosts, as if attending your own funeral, for example.
Imagine, rather, that you no longer exist. The dead do not think, the dead do not feel, the dead do not have desires.

I invite you to explore whether anything remains that is not of this world.

When you hear the cymbals and open your eyes, in a few minutes, try looking with the eyes of one who still lives amongst the dead— from "the afterlife"—as if you were a dead person visiting, and do not belong to the world.

And when you feel like it, approach someone to continue in silence a little while, with that gaze from the beyond.

Let us share a little now, although it seems to me that you do not feel much like talking.

Woman: I connected with when I was 9 years old. I had an accident and was clinically dead. Today I recovered the sense of how good it feels on the other side. I have realized that, for me, the difficult thing is to be in this world and stay connected to that a little.

Claudio: Of course, that is the key.

Woman 2: At first, I felt something like a deep restfulness but then I had to give up, because images of my deceased came to me— in the coffin, and the suffering all around, the crying.

Claudio: Death knows nothing of coffins.

Woman 2: Well, I got very annoyed and gave up.

Woman 3: I felt that I was becoming air and at first it was like a feeling of great happiness because I felt I was becoming part of my family, my ancestors, whom I never knew. Like finally a reunion with a great happiness, a very peaceful feeling, of... at last. Also while all this was happening, images came to me of being wind, a breath—like an air that enters and leaves many different bodies and passes through landscapes as a breath of life.

Claudio: You passed "to a better life" (laughter).

In one of Nasrudin's stories, he comments that babies cry when they are born because they come from a better world and they do not like the one here.

Woman 4: Meeting with her was like ... I liked it.

Claudio: You lived death as going home, it seems.

Woman 5: Well, I died happy, death was happy. It was worth it, and I could let go. When I dissolved, the image would be as if I had connected with a breath that sees.

And then when I opened my eyes, a feeling that I come from the source of love. That I look from the source of love, and it went beyond my partner. Then I was comfortable, complete, and as I slowly came back here, I wanted to cry, because it was too big and I needed to cry because it does not fit inside me.

Claudio: It would seem that the "peace of the dead" is not so inaccessible. It seems to me that the path of death is an alternative to the path of space.

We can become nothing through space, or turn to nothing through death; they are complementary.

Is there anyone who still feels as if they are looking from the other side?

Woman 6: It is as if I am realizing now.

Claudio: We are accustomed to awareness of certain things, and that is like an unconsciousness. One has to disappear to be able to truly remember; and if one tries to remember without forgetting oneself, one "remembers" a "self" that one is not.

Man 1: ... This already happened to me yesterday in the authentic movement session: remaining grounded and with a feeling of plenitude and of peace. And I still have it.

Claudio: Something akin to feeling unalterable matter.

Woman: What I see with this is that it is there and here.

Claudio: Here we are sent to this purgatory to suffer until we learn to find bliss.

What has happened here corresponds to what many people who have experienced a clinical death say. Some return from such experiences with a sense of a mission, feeling that there is something they still have to do.

According to the Tibetan view, only in the human condition (however difficult) can one evolve, and therefore it is preferable to Paradise or the realm of the gods, which is a very blissful condition in which there is no evolution. All cultures agree that it is "here" that work can be done.

Woman 7: It seemed to me that love is something like a translation; a language of this world, as I understand it, which beyond it, is not even called love. What came to me was pure light.

The Eternal Present That We Are

Today I will invite you to do a second experiment, which I learned not from Buddhism but from Eckhart Tolle, and which refers to the direction of time.

We all seem to agree that we move forward in time and that, as we move forward, things are left behind—in a similar way as when one travels on a train the trees are left behind.

However, we have all had an experience that makes us aware of the relativity of movement. Perhaps we have had the experience of being on a train and not knowing if it is our carriage that is moving, or if it is the neighboring train that is moving. Also in an airplane, it sometimes happens that when we cannot clearly feel the engine or the vibration, we do not know if what is moving is what we are looking at, or if it is us moving.

So we may ask ourselves: Is it that we move towards the future, or is it that things are coming to us from the future and then moving towards our past, while "we" are always in the present?

Since it is a matter of perspective—movement being relative—I invite you to experience changing your point of view.

Please adopt the point of view of one who thinks: "I am here, unmoved, while experience passes through me."

Just as we have done with regard to space, when we imagined ourselves to be like the lens through which the drama of a film is passing, let us now think of ourselves as the changeless present through which our experiences are flowing.

It would seem that what we experience comes to us from our future, but it is not that we go toward it.

If I am always in the present, it is my experiences that come to me.

If we can easily switch from our usual point of view to this alternative interpretation of experience, we may be surprised by the discovery that, not only have we always been in the now, but we *are* the Now.

It is as if the here and now were the only stable or permanent thing, for everything else passes through us and the moment in which time is concentrated is empty, which is to say, without contents of its own.

Experiences, thoughts, emotions, and desires are part of a stream that passes through this "here and now" that is in fact eternal and unchanging.

Now I will proceed to reiterate what I have described in the form of a guided meditation.

Just as in the case of a passenger sitting in a carriage, who imagines that it is not the train that is moving, but what he or she sees through the window, let us adopt the perspective that our perceptions pass through our moment in time.

Life passes as a continuous flow through us,
while we ourselves are but an unalterable transparency.

And it continues to be true that one cannot bathe twice
in the same river
when we will adopt the view
that we are simply in the present
which is an eternal present—
while it is the flow of our perceptions that is moving.

Part of our attention captures that things flow,
but we can choose not to look so much at the content of our thoughts,
or our emotions or our desires.
All kinds of experiences flow through us
and there is something painful and perhaps something joyful at
every moment,
but let us pay attention, rather,
to the *field*
through which everything flows,
which is a "here."

Just as when we inverted our perception of figure/background in
regard to space,
the inversion of our perspective with respect to time
also allows us to feel that we are neither
our thoughts nor our perceptions nor other transient
mental states.

Does not our experience confirm what physicists say,
and seem to us so abstract or removed from reality
that we are, fundamentally, space-time?

Clearly this may be experienced with varying degrees of depth,
for we can detach ourselves with greater or lesser depth from what
passes through us.

And possibly we do not yet feel that we are empty
of everything that flows through us
as a pure presence without attributes,
or a pure consciousness.

However, we can understand, at least,
that if we were to perceive it without doubt,
our problems would come to an end.

Let us open our eyes, now,
taking care not to become distracted from what we are doing:
attending to the flow of experiences in the moment,
while remaining a pure permeability or openness,
that is at the same time freedom
and invulnerability.

And then let us also include the perception of the other.

[Gong]

Some Further Advice to My Readers

Having now reached the end of the selection of transcripts of my guided meditations, it seems to me that all I need to finish this book are some words of encouragement so that those who have read it may be stimulated to put such guidance into practice—as those who heard me in person in my courses have done.

To this purpose, it may be useful to share that, in spite of my interest in meditation, it was a long time before I began to practice systematically and that this did not happen until I received what I might call an initiation.

This came from someone who, in spite of not being a recognized instructor, was the bearer of an Indian lineage and thus a bearer of something that went beyond knowledge about how to practice.

At his suggestion, I promised to send him a few lines after each of my daily meditations in the course of the month following our meeting.

The idea was simply that after meditating, I would write something down, either about the apparent results of the meditation or about the apparent lack of results.

Naturally, I discovered through the process that though each of the sessions seemed fairly insignificant, I had quite a few things to say about them. More importantly, however, after a month of fulfilling my commitment to share those notes, I had already made a habit of meditating every morning.

Since then, at the end of my period of work with a group in which meditation is part of the curriculum, when students are about to return home to make the most of our ten days together, during which they have been meditating regularly and thus developing some momentum, I end up advising them to continue the practice for just another week.

Yes, just one more week—always writing something down after each session and being open to the possibility that at the end of that week they might see for themselves whether it was worth committing for another fifteen days.

The formula has worked well because after those fifteen days (preceded by the ten of our meeting plus an extra week), some did not hesitate to commit for a month—and after that some treasure the discipline enough that they have become established meditators.

Although this is a commitment only to themselves that nobody has supervised, it appears that many have come to be constant meditators who have adopted a habit more difficult to establish than it seems.

For it is common that a person setting their mind to this practice will notice all that competes with such a purpose: sleeping in for longer, having to leave the house in a rush, the telephone, different pending tasks, a special kind of mood, an argument with someone that makes the mind too interested in solving an emotional or practical problem, etc., etc.

To meditate means to be willing to give preference to doing nothing in the midst of myriad options to do this or that—and having reached that interest in doing nothing will surely reveal a mind not completely enslaved to its passions and routines.

And while I would say that the sentiment that accompanies this decision is not necessarily devotional, the practical fact of preferring to do nothing in view of the development of one's own mind is implicitly giving preference to an aspiration towards something that is not exactly of this world and therefore, in a broad sense of the term, "an act of spiritual aspiration."

Apart from this advice to establish a habit of meditating for at least half an hour a day, either in the mornings, at the end of the day, or at any other time that is convenient (and a set time is usually more advisable than one which is left open to external circumstances and states), I should advise my readers to systematically use this book, which proposes a practice of Buddhist meditation through the main current schools in the sequence of their historical development.

But these are interpersonal meditations which were explained to people who then sat down in pairs, started their practice with eyes closed, and next explored a silent contact with eyes open.

How can the situation for which these meditations were originally proposed be translated into a solitary context?

My advice is to carry out the exercises in front of a mirror and I will say no more because experience will take care of that.

I will only mention here that this ancient technique is the source of the word "speculation," although the current sense of this term has changed much from the situation that originally inspired it.

I have proposed so far not only to create a habit and a set time for meditation but also a space: a place in front of a mirror with a suitable seat, be it a meditation cushion, a meditation bench, or in some cases a chair (although there are some advantages to adopting some of the basic positions on the floor).

My next advice is to go through this book in the sequence of its pages because the meditations I propose in it derive their effectiveness in part from the way they are ordered.

In addition, my intention to present meditations that correspond to the three most important living schools of Buddhism is inspired by a teaching from the Nyingmapa school (and it was personally helpful to me decades ago to read a small book about this by the yogi C.M. Chen).

Yet how can a person not listening to these meditations remember their stages when practicing them?

Regardless of whether some would like to take brief notes to remember the stages or even combine a summary with the use of a chronometer with a sound signal, I imagine that it is possible to practice the content of each of these meditations after simply making the effort of studying them a little, so as to remember them in the short term.

Should one who does the practice in this way discover that they have omitted something important, it would be worthwhile to repeat the meditation in question on the next day or even more than once. After all, many of the meditations I describe here could be practiced for a whole year with great benefit.

In terms of this project, the meditations I have transcribed here would take between a little more than a month or several months to be put into practice—and I am sure that whoever does so will feel great satisfaction in not having just read another book.

Unfortunately, my commitments and age do not allow me to invite my readers to contact me directly when they encounter serious questions or significant sharing experiences.

I trust, however, that the practice will gradually answer their questions and those who feel drawn to face-to face-contact with a meditation teacher will not find it very difficult to locate one in their area, since Buddhism has reached practically all countries—and now we have Google's search engine too.

I say farewell then to my meditator readers, wishing them constancy in the endeavor and the blessings that come to those who sincerely seek what deserves to be sought.